D0194913

BOOK SALE
Solano College Library

VOYAGES

:(OF THE):

STEAMBOAT

Yellow Stone

ALSO BY DONALD JACKSON

Valley Men: A Speculative Account of the
Arkansas Expedition of 1807

Black Hawk: An Autobiography
(editor)

The Journals of Zebulon Montgomery Pike:
With Letters and Related Documents
(editor)

Custer's Gold: The U.S. Cavalry Expedition of 1874

The Expeditions of John Charles Frémont
(editor, with Mary Lee Spence)

George Washington and the War of Independence

The Diaries of George Washington
(editor, with Dorothy Twohig)

Letters of the Lewis and Clark Expedition:
With Related Documents, 1783–1874
(editor)

Thomas Jefferson and the Stony Mountains:
Exploring the West from Monticello

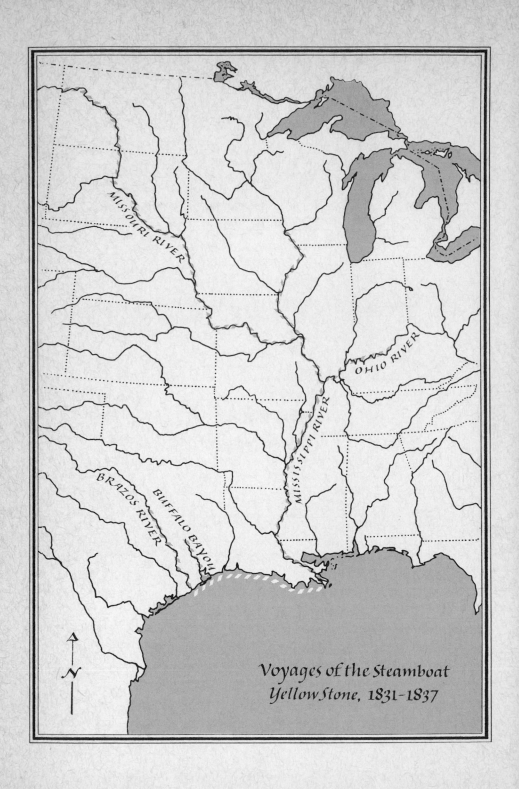

MISSOURI RIVER

OHIO RIVER

MISSISSIPPI RIVER

BRAZOS RIVER

BUFFALO BAYOU

N

Voyages of the Steamboat
Yellowstone, 1831–1837

VOYAGES OF THE STEAMBOAT Yellow Stone

Donald
Jackson

◇

Ticknor & Fields ◇ New York
1985

Copyright © 1985 by Donald Jackson

All rights reserved. No part of this work may be reproduced or transmitted in any form or by any means, electronic or mechanical, including photocopying and recording, or by any information storage or retrieval system, except as may be expressly permitted by the 1976 Copyright Act or in writing from the publisher. Requests for permission should be addressed in writing to Ticknor & Fields, 52 Vanderbilt Avenue, New York, New York 10017.

Library of Congress Cataloging in Publication Data

Jackson, Donald Dean, 1919–

   Voyages of the steamboat Yellow Stone.
   Includes index.
   1. Missouri River — Description and travel. 2. Yellow Stone (Ship). 3. Missouri River Valley — Description and travel. 4. Missouri River — History. 5. Missouri River Valley — History. I. Title.
F598.J32 1985   977.8   85–8048
ISBN 0–89919–306–4

Printed in the United States of America

V 10 9 8 7 6 5 4 3 2 1

For my father
DEAN JACKSON

Contents

Illustrations

MAPS

Preface

◄◌ THE RIVER TURNS from the darkest of grays to a foggy white as morning comes to the Upper Missouri. A steamboat tied to a great cottonwood along the bank bobs slightly as the underbrush gently rubs the hull on one side, and the fast, sandy water scours the other.

The first stirs come from the aft end of the vessel. A dog barks and the cook — the poor old cook, who is always the first out of bed in the army and navy, in cafés and hotels everywhere, and certainly on the riverboats of America — begins his day. Soon he is lobbing a fresh ham off one of the hog carcasses that swing from iron hooks at the stern. What he has in mind for breakfast is fried ham with red-eye gravy, a panful of beaten biscuits, some eggs if the hens in the slatted crates at his feet have been fruitful, and a couple of pots of awesomely gritty coffee. If there are mushrooms to be found on shore, he will send a platter of batter-fried morels up to the officers' table.

Now two firemen for the next shift are up and stretching. The lowest members of the social order among the crewmen, they have slept in most of their clothing on straw pads and buffalo robes in the worst quarters on the main deck. But there is no suggestion of inferiority in their manner as they step to the guard rail to urinate and spit into the water, or as they turn to the stacks of firewood lying close by the boilers, for they know that if they do not move, the vessel does not move. The engineer has lit off the firebox, and soon the firemen will be ramming four-foot lengths of dry oak and ash into the glowing pit while the rest of the crew begins to waken.

In the forward cabin, the captain, pilot, two engineers, the mate, and the clerk will eat their breakfast from ironstone china as they plan the day's run. The sailors in the forecastle will take their meals on wooden trenchers. And the French fur trappers, or *engagés*, living on the main deck as they travel to their summer posts, will eat from communal kettles whatever their own cook has scraped together.

The pilot waits at his station for word from below that the engineer has steam up in the boilers. Glancing at the smoke, now thickening and darkening as it leaves the sheet-iron chimneys, he gauges the "weight" and quality of the steam by the sound in the escapement pipe, while the engineer on the main deck checks the pressure and calls for still more wood. The paddle wheels on either side of the hull move haltingly at first — as the lines are cast off and the boat floats free of the willow brush — then turn smoothly and with great power, thrusting their wooden paddles into the advancing water to move the vessel upstream.

A miracle has happened. Someone has built a fire under a pot of water and it is turning a wheel. It is the 1830s, and the age of steam has come to the uttermost edge of the western American frontier.

Technological advances were always seized upon by the men and women of the frontier, who quickly adopted the steel-shared plow, Colt's revolver, McCormick's mechanical reaper, and barbed wire. Years before these aids to survival came along, however, the pioneers had adopted the steamboat. In the 1830s, the railroad was barely in the picture; a few miles of the first passenger railway, the Baltimore and Ohio, had been laid in 1828, but by that time the steamboat already had been recognized as "the chief technological means by which the wilderness was conquered and the frontier advanced," in the words of economic historian Louis C. Hunter. "Of all the elements of the prosperity of the West," wrote journalist and novelist James Hall, "of all the causes of its rapid increase in population, its growth in wealth, resources and improvements, its immense commerce and gigantic energies, the most efficient has been the navigation by steam."

The noisy and throbbing deck of the steamboat *Yellow Stone* is an excellent platform from which to view the American frontier of this era. Built long before the so-called golden age of the riverboat (it had grown old in service before Mark Twain was born), the *Yellow Stone* plied the Upper Missouri, bringing furs downstream to the markets of the world and carrying goods upriver to Indians who had never heard the roar of an engine. And when her usefulness on the High Plains seemed to be ending, she was shifted to another frontier, to become a part of the history and folklore of the Republic of Texas.

The first decade of real steamboat activity on the Upper Missouri belonged to the fur trade. More precisely, it belonged to the American Fur Company and its St. Louis agents, the men who figure so heavily in this tale. The *Yellow Stone* (always two words in those days) was succeeded over the years by the *Assiniboin,* the *Diana,* the *St. Peters,* the *Antelope* — the list goes on and on. Meanwhile, settlements were creeping up the left bank of the river (left, that is, if we use the customary practice of naming the right and left banks as though we were looking downstream). Also, the pace of government exploration was picking up in the 1830s, and certain Indian tribes were being deposited along the left bank. The Potawatomis, for example, were moved by steamboat from Indiana and Illinois to what is now southwest Iowa. Farther down the river, the region around what is now Kansas City was developing fast, with places like Westport Landing and Independence Landing becoming staging areas for trading expeditions to Santa Fe. By 1838, steamboat travel had become so common, East and West, that safety was an official concern, and the Treasury Department established the Steamboat Inspection Service, requiring that hulls be inspected annually and boilers twice a year.

In the early 1840s, left-bank settlement reached the area of St. Joseph, Missouri, which had for half a century been a fur-trading center. Exploring parties into the far West were led by John Charles Frémont, who made three treks from Westport Landing, the longest taking him to California. The second half of the decade belonged to the Mormons and the Oregon Trail people, seeking a homeland, and then to the gold-rush hordes in search of El Dorado.

The Bidwell-Bartleson party left for Oregon in 1841, having journeyed to Westport Landing by steamboat. Marcus Whitman led the first mass migration of about a thousand persons in 1843, and the Oregon Territory was acquired from the British in 1846. That was the year the first wave of Mormons moved across Iowa to winter quarters on the Missouri, some staying behind to start villages in western Iowa that would become Council Bluffs and Glenwood. Others came upriver by steamboat, using Omaha on the west bank as their point of departure, heading for the Great Salt Lake. The discovery of gold on the American River in California brought more thousands of migrants from the Mississippi Valley in 1849, again traveling by steamboat to jumping-off places such as Westport Landing and St. Joseph. One estimate says that 30,000 hopeful miners left for California that year. Some easterners sailed on clipper ships, preferring to get there entirely by sea or to cut across Panama.

Settlement had pushed upstream to Council Bluffs as the 1850s began, while the town of Omaha was forming across the river to the west. But it was the passage of the Kansas-Nebraska Act in 1854 that opened the right bank to larger settlement. Brownville, Nebraska, and Sioux City, Iowa, and other blank spaces on maps of the Missouri Valley were rapidly filling in. By 1856, the average time for a steamboat trip from St. Louis to Sioux City was slightly less than nine days. During the first half of 1857, more than 130 steamboats stopped at the Brownville landing.

The Pikes Peak gold rush of 1858–59 was largely an affair promoted and engaged in by midwesterners, using Nebraska City as their staging point. Steamboats that carried the miners upriver to the landing in great excitement were waiting to carry them home again when the exuberance quickly died.

In 1852 the government assumed greater responsibility for river safety and steamboat reliability by enacting a law that required the licensing of pilots and engineers. Accidents on the river were frequent and often terrible. Explosions were the most dramatic: when the water in the boiler was low, the metal would overheat, then explode as cooler water was pumped in. Other causes of accidents were the very prevalent snaggings (damage to the hull from tree trunks in the water), fires, and crushing ice jams. Between 1819 and 1825, more than four hundred steamboats were sunk or damaged on the Missouri.

The 1860s began as an era full of hope for the Missouri Valley. Gold strikes in Nevada and Montana fueled the optimism, and settlement pressed upstream as far as Yankton, South Dakota. Two steamboats, the *Chippewa* and the *Key West,* reached Fort Benton, Montana, in 1860. The Civil War created a hiatus during the first half of the decade, and there was little shipping on the Missouri. The cessation was caused in part by the commandeering of boats by the Union army for use as hospitals and transports, but more directly by the success of Confederate sympathizers in disrupting river traffic. The *Sioux City Register* reported in October 1861: "The Missouri river is effectually blockaded by the secessionists in Missouri. . . . We fear we will be put on short rations before spring."

After the war, prosperity resumed. The Montana gold mines made Fort Benton the upper limit of steamboat travel, especially for vessels of a new kind. The so-called mountain boat was designed for the shallows of the upper river (thirty years too late, the crew of the *Yellow Stone* might have said), with a hull so light and flat that it drew as little as eighteen inches of water. The two side wheels had long since been replaced by a single wheel at the stern for easier passage across sandbars and in snag-filled waters.

It was a time of Indian wars and Indian treaties, both of which put the United States government deeper into the business of transporting men and supplies. Soldiers and their gear had to move to such new posts as Fort Berthold, Fort Rice, Fort Sully, and Fort Union. Agencies to administer Indian affairs at the local level — distributing food and other supplies to the tribes — were established for the Blackfeet, the Yankton Sioux, the Lower Brulés, Poncas, and Santees. After the famous Laramie Treaty of 1868, Sioux agencies grew up at Whetstone and Grand River. A whole new trade had begun for steamboat operators, filling government contracts to serve the Indians on the one hand, and supplying the army on the other. When General George A. Custer was defeated at the Little Big Horn in 1876, a shallow-draft stern-wheeler named the *Far West* shoved its way into seemingly impossible places to recover wounded soldiers.

By then, of course, the railroads were making their inexorable approach, mile by mile, across middle America, halting first to bridge the Mississippi, then pausing again on the east bank of the Missouri. Steam power confronted steam power, but it was not an instant clash of two titans. Just as the steamboat had supplemented older modes of travel by keelboat, flatboat, and Conestoga wagon, the steam locomotive worked in conjunction with the steamboat for many years. The Hannibal and St. Joseph railway line reached St. Joseph in 1859; the Burlington and Missouri reached Council Bluffs a decade later; and the Northern Pacific was ready to bridge the Missouri to Bismarck, North Dakota, by 1873.

The age of the steamboat on western waters was seemingly an era of endless resources. There was plenty of wild deer and turkey for the table, water for the crops, and land from the government almost on request. For the steamboat crews, however, there was always a shortage of one natural resource: the wood used to fuel the engine. No matter if the hills on both sides of the valley were bursting with oak and hickory, and the very edges of the river were rank with black willow and cottonwood;

the steamboatman was always convinced that around the next bend he would find not a tree or bush.

In his logbook for an 1841 voyage on the Missouri, Captain Joseph Sire wrote that in the ten years since boats had been operating on the upper river, all the easily accessible wood had vanished, "and unless one takes measures to replenish in advance I would not be surprised if in the future boats will fail . . . because of wood."

A vessel the size of the *Yellow Stone* burned ten cords of wood a day during a normal daylight run. A cord is a stack of wood cut into four-foot lengths, measuring four feet high and eight feet in width. A day's supply for the *Yellow Stone* would just about have fit on a standard railway flatcar of today, and its sheer bulk must have taxed the ingenuity of the crew in finding storage space for it.

In terms of living trees, according to the Department of Forestry at Iowa State University, a cord represents the usable wood in two white oaks sixteen inches in diameter "breast high," and sixty feet tall, with the smaller top branches disregarded. Consider the *Yellow Stone* on a voyage of seventy days to Fort Pierre, and another fifteen days to return to St. Louis helped along by the current. Disregard the fact that the boilers might require less wood going downstream, and that the wood would surely be of various kinds and quality. The amount consumed on this single voyage would have required the equivalent of 1700 oak trees that might have been growing for half a century.

We can estimate that during her lifetime of six and a half years, the *Yellow Stone* spent about two thousand days under way. A total of forty thousand trees were consumed, then, in the sooty firebox of one steamboat.

The figures are impressive, even staggering; but wood is a renewable resource, as paper companies remind us daily in advertisements. An acorn pressed into the soil by the heel of a *Yellow Stone* woodcutter would have become another oak in a couple of generations. In the case of the softer woods, such as willow and cottonwood, the regrowth occurs much faster. Furthermore, the river itself, with its constantly caving banks and meandering current that flooded and killed whole forests in the lowlands, must have destroyed more trees than those required by all the steamboats on the river.

The river traffic did not change the face of the land by the direct consumption of trees so much as by the transporting of settlers who came to stay: the rail-splitters, stump-pullers, saw-mill operators, barn-raisers, and corn-planters. When a farmer cut a tree and pulled the stump, he and his sons and grandsons intended it to stay cut, as they expanded their fields of grain and forage for a growing market.

If settlement was to spread to areas not served by river commerce, the railroads were vital. But finally, it was to be our network of highways, and the trucks that would run on them, that put an end to river traffic. By the twentieth century, the Missouri River that once had been the main source of transportation for the Valley had become partly a blessing and partly a liability. The U.S. Army Corps of Engineers, once occupied with keeping the channel deepened and the snags removed and with building revetments to protect harbors, now turned its attention to flood control, irrigation, electrical-power generation, and the recreational uses of the river. When the Corps built giant dams on the upper river, one element normally found in such dams was left out. The Fort Peck dam in Montana, and the dams called Garrison, Oahe, Fort Randall, and Gavin's Point in the Dakotas — these structures had no locks. A pilot could no longer take his vessel past one of these dams, and none wanted to; the age of steamboating on the Upper Missouri had come and gone.

Like most studies of western American history, this book is about the course of empire. It is also about the effect of a new technology on a westering nation. If it deals with steamboating as a phenomenon and a profession, it deals more precisely with one little side-wheeled vessel named the *Yellow Stone*, toiling its short life away in the fur trade on the Missouri and working on the Brazos to bring about a new republic called Texas; an engine of Manifest Destiny that seemed always to be on the cutting edge of one frontier or another.

ACKNOWLEDGMENTS
◈ AND A ◈
PERSONAL NOTE

◀ MY RELATIONSHIP WITH WESTERN RIVERS goes back to the days of drought in the 1930s, when as an Iowa farm boy I helped my father swim our cattle to an island in the Missouri where they could forage on willow leaves. But my interest in river navigation, particularly by steam, was not to be quickened for another thirty years.

As a guest of the Federal Barge Lines of St. Louis, in the fall of 1956, I spent some days aboard the *Buna,* a towboat operating on the Mississippi above the lock and dam at Alton, Illinois. As a historian and writer, my purpose then was to observe changes in the Mississippi and her shores during the preceding century and a half. It was not my thought or intention to fall in love with steamboating. The *Buna* was not even a typical old-timer. Her powerful four-cylinder triple-expansion Fulton steam engines drove twin propellers, not paddle wheels. She drew nine feet of water and shoved untold cubic yards of grain and other cargo before her, on barges, with 2800 horsepower. But life aboard was not so different from the way it must have been on the *Yellow Stone.* The pilot knew the river foot by foot. The cook produced incredibly large meals three times daily, calling in the crew with the traditional bell. The crewmen ate silently, prodigiously, then returned to the red-hot engine room in the depths of the vessel, or to the risky catwalks on the barges, far out ahead of the boat.

The *Buna*, built during World War II, is old now. She serves as the office boat for the Cairo, Illinois, fleet of Federal Barge Lines and its parent company. Her pilot house and after cabin are gone, and I am sure that her engine room, converted to office space, now hums with air conditioning, the whirr of electric pencil sharpeners, and perhaps the quiet grinding of a word-processor or two. But for a few days she was my *Yellow Stone*, and I might have been Prince Maximilian himself, a century earlier, sunning himself on the vibrating deck and scribbling in his journals about the wonders of a great river. I thank the *Buna*, and her crew and owners, for that experience.

My gratitude goes also to these persons and institutions, named here alphabetically and not always in the order of their contribution to this endeavor.

Alan Lawrence Bates, steamboat historian and model-builder, who knows much about early boats and their fixed and moving parts. James R. Bentley, secretary of the Filson Club in Louisville, Kentucky, for prompt and useful photocopies, always accompanied by a bit more information than I thought he had. The sponsors and curators of the museum steamboats *William M. Black*, Dubuque, Iowa; *Meriwether Lewis*, Brownville, Nebraska; and *George M. Verity*, Keokuk, Iowa, for a taste of how it must have been.

Joan G. Caldwell, Howard-Tilton Memorial Library of Tulane University, who helped with Thomas Toby & Brother, and with Harrod & Hughes. Carroll Coleman for wise speculation on the printing equipment of Gail Borden and his associates. The staff of the Colorado College Library, who gave me their services and encouraged my work with interest.

The Daughters of the Republic of Texas, whose librarians — especially Sharon Crutchfield and Bernice Strong — were constantly alert to my needs. John R. Ewers, for knowing so much about early Western art and for helping me to find it. The staff of the Fort Lewis College Library and the Center for Southwest Studies, at Durango, Colorado.

Kenneth R. Hall, Judicial, Fiscal, and Social Branch of the National Archives, who found what he could in the ship enrollment records and talked me out of fruitless searching for the rest. Margaret Swett Henson, wise in Texas history. Jane Hogan, who searched her late husband's papers for me.

Joan and Chester Kerr, who thought that telling the *Yellow Stone* story was not a bad idea. Sara Dunlap Jackson, archivist at the National Historical Publications and Records Commission, for thirty years of patience with me and thousands of other historians. Janet Lecompte who, as a fellow Colorado Springs writer, shares information and enthusiasm with me on nearly a daily basis.

Harold D. Moser, editor of *The Papers of Andrew Jackson*, who followed up a hunch of mine that did not work out. The staff of the Missouri Historical Society, St. Louis, including executive director Raymond F. Pisney, former archivist Beverly Bishop, director of museum programs Gary N. Smith, and Peter Michel. Allan L. Montgomery at the Bertrand Conservation Laboratory, U.S. Fish and Wildlife Service, near Missouri Valley, Iowa. His *Bertrand* was snagged and sunk in 1865, but his work of interpreting her life and times goes on today.

Joseph C. Porter, curator of Western history, Joslyn Museum, Omaha, and his administrative assistant Marilyn Shanewise; and William C. Orr, who is co-editor with Porter of the forthcoming Maximilian diaries. Their expertise on Maximilian and Bodmer and the generosity of the InterNorth Art Foundation, which owns that material, have been essential.

William H. Rice, Jr., of the Inland Waterways Division of Pott Industries, Inc., for recent information about the *Buna*. William H. Richter, assistant archivist at the Barker Texas History Center at Austin, who always meant it when he offered all the help I might need. James P. Ronda, who curiously respects my work as much as I respect his.

William D. Sawyer, for the use of his drawing of a western steamboat engine. Ernestine Ernst Seiter, of Lexington, Missouri, for letters of James Aull. William L. Talbot, of Keokuk, Iowa, the first steamboat buff I ever met.

My thanks go also to the staffs of the museums, societies, and organizations that have provided pictorial materials.

VOYAGES

‡(OF THE)‡

STEAMBOAT

Yellow Stone

The first night's cruise of the *Yellow Stone* is seen in this painting by George Catlin.
The background is an early view of the St. Louis waterfront.

1

A New Sound in the Valley

❧ THE WINTER HAD BEEN HARD, as most St. Louis winters are. Housebound diarists wrote that the snow was the deepest they had ever known. Wagons crisscrossed the Mississippi on the ice. Just upstream, where the Missouri River came in from the west, buffalo carcasses from the plains had swirled into backwater pools and lay stiffly locked, awaiting a thaw. Now it was mid-April of 1831 with the ice mostly gone, maple buds swelling all over town, and housewives along Kingshighway eyeing their garden plots with a view to the first planting.

Pierre Chouteau, Jr., had missed the worst of the winter. As western agent for the American Fur Company, he had spent the season in New York, dining with the Astors and getting his goods in order for the year's Indian trade. He had come home by stage as far as Louisville, where he had taken possession of his new jewel, the steamboat *Yellow Stone*. Now he stood proudly at the bow, surrounded by a crush of workmen with last-minute cargo, crewmen anxiously getting up steam, and passengers — most of whom had some connection with the company. Up in the pilothouse, Charles La Barge was easing the vessel slowly back from the landing. A notable voyage was beginning.

St. Louisans were accustomed by now to the sights and sounds of steamboat traffic, but this departure was worth a second look to strollers at wharfside. The destination of the *Yellow Stone* was Fort Union, the American Fur Company's trading post far, far up the Missouri, and the vessel was the first steamboat to attempt such a trip. Her two decks were teeming with travelers, who were producing more of a clangor than the ship's bell. Most of the revelers were *engagés* — French employees of the company with surnames like Sibille, Primeau, and Gagnier — who could scarcely stop roistering and chanting Creole songs long enough for the company clerk to check their names in his account book. Each was certified to be a United States citizen and thus entitled to trade in the Indian country. Those on the upper or boiler deck were firing their rifles into the air; others had collapsed in the sun to sleep off last night's frolic, their final one until their return home in the fall. In their own patois, they were not going in search of the beaver, otter, muskrat, and fox, but of the *castor, loutre, rat musqué,* and *renard,* and the item now growing more important to the trade, the buffalo robe — *peaux-de-buffle* — which Americans were demanding to cover their floors, warm their bodies during sleigh rides, and provide handsome overcoats. *Mangeurs du lard,* or pork-eaters, the Frenchmen called themselves, for occasionally there was a gobbet of salt pork in their diet of ground corn and lard.

The capacity of the *Yellow Stone* was great, considering that she was only 120 feet long, twenty feet in the beam, and with a hold just six feet deep. Not only was she carrying all the supplies needed to sustain the men at the trading posts (including perhaps a thousand gallons of whisky), and all the goods for trade with the Indians in return for skins and furs; she had, in addition, ninety-seven men aboard. Of these, twenty-two were crew members and most of the others either *engagés* or company officials. There may have been an Indian agent or two or a young army officer and his wife going up to Cantonment Leavenworth. Even the vessel's fuel was burdensome, for her normal day's consumption of ten cords of wood weighed forty tons if it was oak, twenty-five if it was cottonwood.

———❖———

Perhaps by now Chouteau had begun to think that he had personally conceived the idea of building a steamboat for the upper river trade. The idea, however, had come from Kenneth McKenzie, who ran the Upper Missouri Outfit from Fort Union and was an innovative man. He had written Chouteau late in the summer of 1830 to propose the acquisition of the vessel (later he would name his favorite buffalo horse Steamboat), and Chouteau had tried the proposal on his colleagues before sending it to the home office in New York. The reaction had been mixed. Daniel Lamont strongly supported the plan. Jean Pierre Cabanné and Bernard Pratte were against it, declaring it *un dépense pour un rien,* a needless expense. Cabanné had written from his post at Council Bluff, "It will spare great expense and vexations that are caused by the *engagés,* but as I am no longer young I sometimes worry unreasonably." And then, as if he knew he was fighting a losing cause, he wrote again to Chouteau, "If the steamboat comes up, send me several gallons of good Madeira wine or port. That is all I need."

When Chouteau wrote the home office, he told manager Ramsay Crooks that a steamboat would be safer than a keelboat, and the kind of crew it required would be easier to handle than the unruly *engagés* who poled the keelboats. If there was one drawback, it was the danger of mechanical breakdown, so Chouteau proposed to have spare parts and a blacksmith on board. "We could keep all our men in the Indian country, where we could pay the greater part of their wages in merchandise instead of making the larger outlay of cash which we are now constantly required to do. In the off season, the boat could be put to work in warmer waters. It should cost about $7000, with spare parts and extras adding another thousand."

The New York office bought the idea. Louisville was chosen as the building site (see Appendix A for construction details), and by the time of delivery everyone involved was convinced that the plan was a splendid one. On 16 April 1831, the *St. Louis Beacon* reported:

A new and handsome steam boat, belonging to the American Fur Company, arrived in this port on Sunday last and proceeds to-day, it is understood, for the mouth of the Yellow Stone. . . . Should the company succeed in reaching this point with their boat, we have good reasons for believing that success will repay them for all the expense, and toil, and risk, which must necessarily attend them; and we shall have the pleasure of beholding what, it was thought the other day, was reserved for the next generation.

And to William B. Astor in the home office, senior partner Pratte sent off the happy message: "Le steamboat Yellow Stone a laissé le port le 16 à midi."

THE FIRST CREW

Plenty of men in the St. Louis area were capable of operating a steamboat. Several other boats had scheduled voyages on the lower Missouri that year: The *Globe* was going to Leavenworth at the mouth of the Kansas River; the *Liberty* and the *Missouri* were bound for Liberty, Missouri. The *Chieftain* would make several ports on the lower river. There also was a thriving traffic on the Mississippi.

It seems likely, however, that most of the first *Yellow Stone* crew was hired in Louisville. As she was brought to St. Louis under steam, apparently with some freight and passengers, she probably arrived well staffed. Surviving lists of crew members for 1831 and 1832 tell us something of crewmen and their duties.

THE MASTER OR CAPTAIN

Benjamin Young, probably from the Ohio River Valley, has left us little information about himself, except that in 1845 a captain named Young would make the fastest time on record in taking the *Monona* from St. Louis to Galena, Illinois, on the Upper Mississippi. The captain was in general charge of the vessel, and

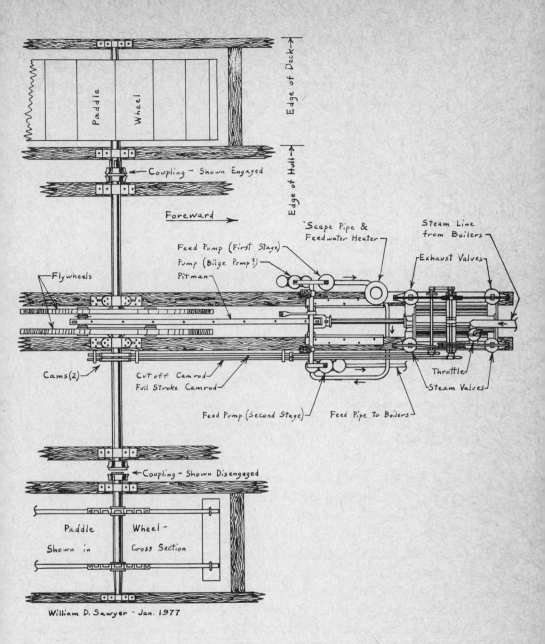

Steam cylinder, flywheels, and paddle wheels are vital components in this
drawing of a high-pressure steamboat engine of the *Yellow Stone*'s day.

some were trained to double as pilots; all were businessmen, for each steamboat was a fiscal entity of its own. When a crate of chickens was brought aboard the *Yellow Stone*, it was charged to the boat. When a traveler booked passage, the fare went into the coffers of the vessel, not of the American Fur Company. Captain Young strode the decks like a naval captain at sea, trying to make the best possible time without endangering his vessel. Instead of a panoply of gleaming instruments and gauges on a panel in the pilot house, he had two sounds to guide him: the roar of the draft in the two blackened chimneys (never called smokestacks) and the popping of steam as it left the escapement pipes in a succession of ear-splitting explosions that dissolved in the air above the top deck.

The captain also kept the log, recording the mileage, stops for wood, groundings and other mishaps, and any untoward event on board or ashore. No log of the *Yellow Stone* has survived, but it must have been similar to the logs of vessels of later periods. Captain Joseph Sire, aboard the company's *Nimrod* in 1844, made this entry on 13 May: "The rain continues through the night — we are soon at the Pratte Cut-off — we are taking soundings and in the meantime I am having some wood gathered. We find also a cut made in the large bar below Blackbird Hill. Since there is much driftwood I stop to have it cut. Camped at eight-thirty o'clock about four miles below the prairie of the Omaha village [in present-day Nebraska]."

THE MATE

John Rodgers served as mate on this voyage, with the responsibility of managing the deckhands, relieving the captain on watch, and generally acting as second in command.

THE FIRST AND SECOND ENGINEERS

The first engineer was Joseph Postlethwaite and the second a man named Lovejoy. Postlethwaite could sign his name, as indicated by a few vouchers he endorsed in St. Louis, but the job of engineer was not one requiring much education or experience. Most of the adjusting of the engine — such as the setting of the cutoff cams and the marking of the safety valve lever to denote a dangerous build-up of steam — had been done by the manufacturer. It was necessary, however, for an engineer to be on the alert in case the pilot called for more or less steam or for the disengagement of one or both paddle wheels for a tricky maneuver. After a day's run, the fires were extinguished and the mud-valves on the giant boilers opened for draining. The turbid water of the Missouri, which was considered "all right to drink if you have some other water to wash it down with," deposited scale that had to be chipped away daily. The engineer kept a low profile; usually he was out of sight, oiling and cleaning, repacking the cylinder, coaxing the engine to greater performance, watching for cracked pipes and leaking joints, and responding to signals from the pilothouse.

THE PILOT

In 1831 and again in 1832, the pilot of the *Yellow Stone* was Charles S. La Barge, of St. Louis, whose long career on the river would last until 1852, when he would die in the explosion of the *Saluda*. The company account books carried entries for La Barge as early as 1824, when, as the firm's top *patron* or steersman-manager of a keelboat crew, he had made many trips on the Missouri. His younger brother, Joseph, was to become a chronicler of life on the river; his active imagination and uncertain recall of facts will be dealt with later in this work.

Although the pilot's job is the easiest to describe, it was the most difficult to perform. He had to know what was happening at all times aboard the vessel and in the river ahead. He had to remember which cutoff he had risked using on his last trip, bearing in mind that it might not be there now. He had to know a dozen ways to get off a sandbar and how to ease his boat through a field of snags whose great, bare branches were either thrust into the air or lurking just below the water. He had to know from the sound of the escapement pipe whether he had called for too much steam or not enough. Upon awakening in his quarters and peering out his window, after being spelled off by his steersman, he had to be able to tell exactly where he was: just leaving the chute behind Morgan's Island; just coming up on

Calumet Bluff; running ahead of schedule, but with a falling river. In later years when night running became common, he would need to distinguish between the different darknesses of the water, the sky, and the bluffs on the dim horizon.

THE STEERSMAN

To relieve the pilot at the wheel, and to go out in the yawl and make soundings of the river bottom, the *Yellow Stone* carried a steersman. In 1831 it was Toussaint Petre.

THE CARPENTER

So many vital parts of the steamboat were made of wood — the pitman rod, flywheel, paddle wheels, rudder, and spars — that a carpenter was always busy. Frank Young was this important crewman in 1831. No blacksmith is listed for this voyage, although Chouteau had planned to carry one. No doubt the engineers were good amateur smiths.

THE SAILORS

This is the term in the records for what must have been roustabouts, deckhands, and general laborers. In 1831 these were Henry Hugo, James Anderson, David Ross, and James Mitchill.

THE STEWARD AND THE CABIN BOY

Patrick Lane and J. Daniel held these jobs on the 1831 voyage. Their roles would become more important in future years, when extra berthing space for passengers was added to the boiler deck of the *Yellow Stone*.

THE COOKS

Food for the 1831 voyage was prepared by G. W. Woddington and his assistant, John Woodson. It was ample and satisfying. The cooks or steward bought fresh milk, chickens, eggs, and live hogs while passing through the settled part of the country. They fished off the stern and ranged the hills for venison and bear meat, aided by the expert hunters among the *engagés*. The hold carried such staples as flour and beans, barrels of salt pork, and special delicacies required by Chouteau himself.

THE FIREMEN

The six firemen in 1831 were: David Brown, James Jackson, John Hinds, Richard Foster, Antoine Latreille, and Joe Alfred. The work was so arduous that at least three shifts were required. In feeding wood into the cavernous fireboxes below the boilers, the men were exposed alternately to the searing blast of the fire and — as they returned to the woodpile for another log — the damp chill of the river air. The danger of carrying wood across a slippery deck, perhaps too soon after the daily issuance of the whisky ration, was another hazard.

A question not fully answered by the documents in the surviving papers is whether the firemen were black or white, slave or free. During construction of the vessel, a supervisor wrote Chouteau about the necessity of providing separate quarters for the firemen. And while they are listed by full name on the 1831 crew list, by 1832 they are listed by first name only. Diarist Stephen Hempstead, Sr., is known to have hired his slaves out to riverboat captains. "My Negro man Tom came home from the Steam Boat Diana from Louisville," he wrote in 1831.

———————◆———————

These social distinctions and divisions of labor meant little to the man at the top. John Jacob Astor owned ships that plied the great seas from London to Calcutta and Canton and even north to Siberia. Now he owned the little *Yellow Stone* and, in a sense, all the men aboard her. He very nearly owned the fur trade, although there were holdouts, tough old-timers with their little outfits, taking what was left. This man who had come to America as a poor immigrant was now striking medals with his image on one side, in imitation of the United States government, as a kind of coinage with which to impress the Indians who supplied his furs.

Historian Bernard DeVoto seemed to have Astor in mind when he wrote of "the tendency of twentieth-century historians to hold the eighteen-thirties in American history to ideas which the eighteen-thirties had never heard of, which they would not have understood, and which produce confusion and nonsense when imposed on them today." If there was avarice in Astor's methods, there was also audacity. He had sent his agents by sea

ENROLMENT.

Nº 104

Enrolment, *In conformity to an Act of the Congress of the* **UNITED STATES OF AMERICA,** *entitled "An Act, for enrolling and licensing Ships or Vessels to be employed in the coasting trade and fisheries, and for regulating the same."*

Patrick McCarthy of the City of New Orleans acting as agent for the owners.

having taken or subscribed the *Oath* required by the said Act, and having *Sworn* that *the Company known by the Name & Stile of the "American Fur Company" whereof William B Astor of the City of New York is President and which Company is incorporated under the Authority of the United States.*

I are Citizen of the **UNITED STATES,** sole owner of the ship or vessel, called the *Yellow Stone* of *St Louis* whereof *A. G. Bennett* is at present Master, and as he hath *Sworn* is a Citizen of the UNITED STATES, and the said ship or vessel was *built at Louisville in the State of Kentucky in this present Year 1831*

AND *L. B. Willis, acting Surveyor of the port of New Orleans* **HAVING CERTIFIED,** that the said ship or vessel has *one* deck and *no* mast and that her length is *One hundred & twenty two feet, one Inch* her breadth *Twenty feet, Six Inches* her depth *Six feet, one Inch* and that she measures *One hundred forty four and 8/95th* TONS: that she has a *Steam boat* has a *Square Stern, two Chimneys & two Cabins* and an *Alligator* head: And the said *Patrick McCarthy* having agreed to the description and admeasurement above specified, and sufficient security having been given according to the said act, the said *Steam boat* has been duly enrolled at the **PORT OF ORLEANS.**

GIVEN *under our hands and seal, at the* PORT OF ORLEANS, *this Fifth day of November in the year one thousand eight hundred and Thirty one*

First licensing of the new American Fur Company steamboat as she was prepared for service on the Upper Missouri.

and land to the mouth of the Columbia, nearly on the heels of Lewis and Clark, to establish the short-lived trading post called Astoria. He had almost single-handedly — with the help of a few friends in Congress — killed the government's factory system, which since 1795 had been sponsoring trading houses for the Indians. "Unfair!" cried Astor and such expansionists as Senator Thomas Hart Benton, of Missouri — and the factory system had died in 1822.

Now, Astor could price his goods at obscene levels, ranging from 200 to 2000 percent above cost, arguing that he had to pay a heavy customs duty that his British competitors did not; that he must maintain a larger number of employees than the trade required, to protect his posts from the wilder Indians; and that the supply of furs was finite and diminishing.

The imminent death of the fur trade was a part of the Astor paranoia. "The account which you give of the trade is gloomy indeed," he wrote to Ramsay Crooks a few weeks before he sold 550,000 muskrat skins at thirty-six cents each, reserving 200,000 for future sale. The other near-paranoid aspect of the Astor psyche was the notion that every other trader, even the poor devil who tramped the watercourses of the West alone to bring in a pitifully small pack of beaver skins in the spring, was somehow a deadly enemy. Astor's solution for competitive traders large and small? Buy the rascals out.

By 1825 the cutthroat trade had fed upon itself until Astor's chief competitors were Bernard Pratte & Company in St. Louis and the Columbia Fur Company on the Upper Missouri. These two firms were bringing almost all the beaver pelts and buffalo robes to St. Louis, and had to be dealt with. First, Astor bought out Pratte & Company in 1827, agreeing to accept that company's furs and sell them on commission and to provide trade goods at a specified markup above New York and London prices.

Having got the Pratte company, including the influential and energetic Pierre Chouteau, Jr., in his pocket, Astor moved on the Columbia Fur Company, the central figure of which was Kenneth McKenzie. A Scotsman who had entered the trade from

Canada, McKenzie already had built Fort Tecumseh near the site of present-day Pierre, South Dakota, and other posts as far down the Missouri as Council Bluff.

When McKenzie's company gave in to Astor's pressure, it became known as the Upper Missouri Outfit, to be supervised by Pratte & Company. Both these entities fell under the general heading of the Western Department, to be distinguished from the Northern Department on the Upper Mississippi and in the Great Lakes region. McKenzie and his three associates, William Laidlaw, James Kipp, and Daniel Lamont, agreed to confine their activities to the Upper Missouri and the area west to the Rocky Mountains.

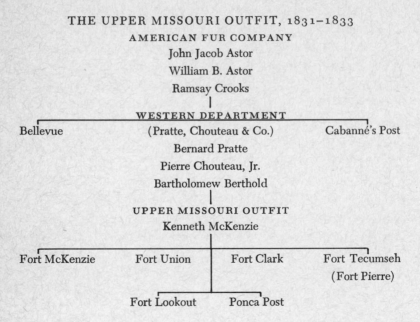

THE UPPER MISSOURI OUTFIT, 1831–1833

AMERICAN FUR COMPANY
John Jacob Astor
William B. Astor
Ramsay Crooks

WESTERN DEPARTMENT

Bellevue	(Pratte, Chouteau & Co.)	Cabanné's Post
	Bernard Pratte	
	Pierre Chouteau, Jr.	
	Bartholomew Berthold	

UPPER MISSOURI OUTFIT
Kenneth McKenzie

Fort McKenzie	Fort Union	Fort Clark	Fort Tecumseh (Fort Pierre)

Fort Lookout	Ponca Post

The dreams of all these men and their scores of employees were vested in their flagship. Looking back, it might be said that the *Yellow Stone*, so eagerly cheered on her first voyage by St. Louis newspapers and by all who knew about her and wished her well, was a kind of pirate ship.

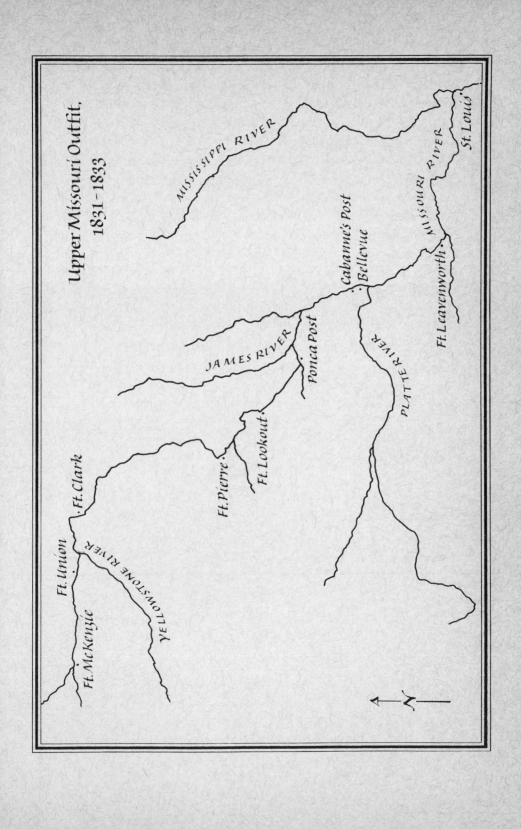

Upper Missouri Outfit,
1831–1833

MISSISSIPPI RIVER

Cabanné's Post
Bellevue

St. Louis

MISSOURI RIVER

Ft. Leavenworth

JAMES RIVER

Ponca Post

PLATTE RIVER

Ft. Lookout

Ft. Pierre

Ft. Clark

Ft. Union

YELLOWSTONE RIVER

Ft. McKenzie

N

Between St. Louis and Cantonment Leavenworth, near the mouth of the Kansas River, was a stretch of 425 miles dotted with little settlements and well known to boatmen. The capital of Missouri had been moved west to Jefferson City in 1826 and still contained no more than a scattering of small buildings and the first legislative hall. Many of the settlements —St. Charles, Franklin, Boonville, Lexington, Liberty — were much older and all were growing faster now that a steamboat trade had been established.

Because the stretch of water between St. Louis and St. Charles was so much traveled and so well charted in the minds of captains and pilots, it already had become customary for steamboats to leave St. Louis in daylight, run all night, and arrive at the St. Charles landing about dawn. A road leading across the countryside provided an alternate route for passengers bound only for St. Charles or for express riders hurrying to catch the boat before it got out of range. But from St. Charles on, steamboats would not travel during the hours between deep dusk and dawn.

A day's schedule might look like this:

4:00 A.M. Firemen lighting off fires, engineer getting up steam.

DAYLIGHT. Sailing time.

6:30 A.M. Breakfast (each meal announced by the ship's bell). Sometimes served before departure.

MIDMORNING. Woodcutting stop.

12:30 P.M. Dinner, the heartiest meal of the day.

MIDAFTERNOON. Lying to for woodcutting, boiler cleaning. Fires put out, ash pits emptied into river. Hunters foraging. Engineers servicing the engine — oiling, polishing, repairing.

7:00 P.M. OR LATER. Supper and early bedtime.

On the lower river there was little need for the crew or the *engagés* to cut wood. The day of the woodhawk had arrived, and men would establish themselves near the river and offer stacks of firewood to the steamboats. If the proprietor was not in evidence when the vessel nosed in to shore, the captain sent a party to take on a few cords, measured carefully by the mate with the aid of an eight-foot rule. Then the captain would fire a gun to signal the woodhawk that he could be paid if he appeared. Failing that, he would receive his pay on the return voyage.

By 29 April the *Yellow Stone* was approaching Jack's Ferry at the landing near Lexington. Finding a quantity of cordwood unattended, Captain Young had several cords brought on board. He failed to find the owner, who in fact was not a woodhawk and had cut the fuel for his own use. So, Young backed away and continued upstream. As the St. Louis office was to learn later in a letter written by Lexington merchant James Aull, the wood was the property of a "poor man," Henry Rowland, who wanted payment of $13.50 for nine cords. The company sent word later in the summer that the *Yellow Stone* would settle for seven cords at $10.50. That was not enough, Rowland complained, but he accepted it anyway.

This part of the river was quite familiar to Chouteau, although it had been years since he had traveled it extensively. There had been changes since his boyhood: now he saw dilapidated, used-up structures everywhere, old shacks built by the Spanish before the Louisiana Purchase of 1803, roofless cabins erected by settlers who had gone back east.

While still in his teens, Chouteau had come this way to spend a winter trading with the Osages. Then he had lived for a couple of years in the lead-mining region far up the Mississippi. By the age of twenty-four he had started a mercantile business in St. Louis with his brother-in-law, Bartholomew Berthold. Now forty-three, Chouteau was one of the most powerful men in the West, with an uncanny ability to deal with men of all stations in a way that advanced his own interests. One other characteristic made him a natural partner of the Astors — amoral ruthlessness in matters of business.

His methods were simple. Keep the business in the family as much as possible. Buy out competitors lock, stock, and barrel when they fail, leaving them not so much as a rifle or canoe to help them start again. Follow the letter of the law only when

Ramsay Crooks traveled to the Pacific Coast for John Jacob Astor before becoming manager of his giant fur trading empire.

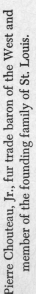

Pierre Chouteau, Jr., fur trade baron of the West and member of the founding family of St. Louis.

another course would hurt business. Do not bother to open up new territory; move in on someone else's. And remember that the word *competitor* is too mild for others who are trading with the Indians. These men are the Opposition.

All this charm and guile were combined in the body of a handsome, black-haired Frenchman who would have been resplendent in a general's uniform had he not chosen the dark suits and white linens of a merchant prince. Although he spoke French most of the time and wrote his letters in that language, he was also fluent in English. That was one part of his adaptability. Another was his readiness to leave a mansion in St. Louis and spend weeks on the Missouri, inspecting an empire that consisted of illiterate compatriots, volatile Indians, trading posts that were scarcely more than hovels, and thousands of square miles of river watershed so empty of the Opposition that it might as well have belonged to him personally.

On the first of May he wrote to General Pratte — a venerable partner in the St. Louis office whose military rank dated back to militia service in the War of 1812 — that the *Yellow Stone* had arrived just below the mouth of the Kansas the night before. There he had found Baptiste Dufond waiting. Listed as "second pilot" in the ship's records, Dufond had come down from Fort Union to pilot the *Yellow Stone* on up the river that he knew so well. Whether first pilot Charles La Barge returned home then, or whether Dufond merely rode along to advise him about the treacheries of the upper river, we do not know. The new pilot was half Chippewa and may never have guided a steamboat before, but he knew keelboat travel and the vessel was in good hands.

———◈———

In 1832 Leavenworth would be given the more permanent designation of "fort," but for now it was a cantonment, one of the westernmost military posts in the United States and the place where the advance of "civilization" seemed to have faltered. Beyond its wooden barracks, stables, and officers' homes overlook-

ing the Missouri, a few miles above the mouth of the Kansas, no
men ventured except Indians, government agents, and traders.
But here one could dine handsomely, sip Madeira, and watch a
regiment of troops at evening parade. To Chouteau the post
meant two things. It was a display of American power that kept
the Indians under control, but also it was an irritating inspection
stop, designated by the government as the place beyond which
no alcoholic beverages could be hauled upriver for sale to the
Indians. Fortunately, the officers at the post were never hard
pressed by their superiors back East and had become lax about
inspecting traders' goods for contraband liquor.

The *Yellow Stone* reached the cantonment on a day in early
May, and the next morning she was gone, her cursory inspection
completed, the social amenities with the officers carried off with
Chouteau's usual aplomb. In the hold of his boat the kegs and
barrels of Monongahela whisky, peach brandy, cherry bounce,
and fiery, concentrated spirits of wine rode secure and unmo-
lested.

The Black Snake Hills would be the next sign of human habi-
tation. Near today's St. Joseph, Missouri, the hills were the location of old Joseph Robidoux's trading house. Robidoux was in
and out of business with Chouteau, never hesitating to go off on
ventures of his own. Here Chouteau may have decided to ask
Captain Young to make his stop as brief as possible, to prevent
the *engagés* from taking advantage of their last reasonable
chance to desert.

The *Yellow Stone* had traveled about 475 miles from the
mouth of the river, and if Chouteau had by now evaluated the
problems of steamboat navigation, he may have reduced them
to matters of underwater obstructions — snags and sandbars —
and the constant, roaring hunger of the great fireboxes. As for
the shallowness of the stream, next year he would begin the trip
three weeks earlier and take advantage of the first spring rise, as
rains and melting snows poured into the channel. That would
give him more water, but, he would learn, not nearly enough.

Often the snags were whole trees that had slid into the water, their roots settling into the mud while their lighter trunks stayed at the surface. "They appear," scientist Joseph N. Nicollet said on his Missouri voyage of 1839, "like a forest of monsters armed with pikes and pitchforks rising ten or fifteen feet above the water." John James Audubon would later add another picturesque description, saying that the snags "show their brittle prongs as if some thousands of mammouth Elk Horns had been planted everywhere for the purpose of impeding navigation." Often it was necessary to saw the snags off under water, one branch at a time.

Farther up the river, the snags would disappear as the wood thinned out. But when the great trees vanished there would be far less fuel, inferior kinds of wood, for the fireboxes. No wood-hawks had come up this far in 1831. Captain Sire would find them in the spring of 1841 about three days' steaming above Leavenworth. But for now, Captain Young would send all able-bodied men ashore at the end of the day's run to look for sound, dry wood. Lacking hearty logs of oak, hickory, or ash, they would take anything, including sandbar willow, cottonwood, and the nondescript driftwood that the river had racked up along the shore. Dry driftwood burned well and made good steam. Wet driftwood had to be coaxed along with handfuls of rosin to make it burn.

Chouteau had called upon his partner, Jean Pierre Cabanné, to help with the wood problem. Cabanné, married to the sister of Chouteau's wife, was wintering at his post a few miles above the Platte and just below the Council Bluff, an area eventually to become a part of Omaha, Nebraska. As early as 21 February, Chouteau had written to ask that he store a supply of wood above and below his post. Cabanné replied that he would have several cords stacked at the mouth of the Platte and farther down at Weeping Water Creek. He would send another crew up the river to cut at the mouth of the Little Sioux.

As no logbook survives and no passengers were keeping journals, the exact schedule of the *Yellow Stone* on this first trip is unknown. We cannot say when the boat stopped at the company post called Bellevue, eight miles above the Platte, or when it reached Cabanné's place several miles farther on. Near his establishment were the remains of an abandoned army post called Fort Atkinson. It was to this post that Major Stephen H. Long, of the Corps of Topographical Engineers, had pioneered by bringing the experimental steamboat *Western Engineer* in 1819. Five years later a single commercial steamboat, the *Mandan*, had come to Fort Atkinson with the usual difficulty of snags and fuel. Indian agent Benjamin O'Fallon had become so impatient that he had traveled the last fifty miles by land. Since that time, no steamboat had tried to make the trip.

The country above Council Bluff was new in other ways, for above this point the landscape changed. The timber on the hills was more sparse and there was less underbrush. In the river the snags were fewer but the sandbars were trickier, the shallows appearing more unexpectedly.

In mid-May the *Yellow Stone* was stopped by low water near the mouth of Ponca Creek, where the company had a small post. Word was sent up to Fort Tecumseh that two keelboats should come downstream to lighten the steamboat by taking off some cargo. But Chouteau and his crew were still mired in the sandy shallows at the end of May, and he sent a letter downriver to Cabanné. "I am sorry you did not warn us about the wisdom of this trip but it would be hard to believe that we would find only 4 to 4½ feet of water at this season. I have sent for boats and hope we can return by them to the Fort." Chouteau added an irascible comment about the Ponca station itself. "This is the most miserable post on the Missouri." He wrote to St. Louis on the same day, telling General Pratte: "This is an unusual season and voyageurs say they have never seen the river this low. All these difficulties do not change my opinion of the value of the steamboat, but they need many improvements."

There was nothing much wrong with the *Yellow Stone* except that she drew too much water. It would take the company many years to realize how shallow the draft of an Upper Missouri steamboat had to be.

Bellevue, shown here in a painting by Karl Bodmer, was for decades a fur trading post located below present-day Omaha.

The most restless man at Fort Tecumseh was not William Laidlaw, the resident manager, but Kenneth McKenzie, who had come all the way from Fort Union to meet the boat — his boat, in a way — at this place. By now the thought must have occurred to both men — and to those on the vessel — that if the crew had experienced so much trouble in getting the *Yellow Stone* this far, urging her on to Fort Union might prove to be an impossible mission.

McKenzie could not wait. He and John F. A. Sanford, subagent for the Mandans, headed downstream to "rescue" the *Yellow Stone*. Taking two keelboats, they met the vessel and all hands turned to off-loading the cargo of blankets, traps, powder and lead, tomahawks, beads, vermilion, pots and pans, and all the trade items now considered de rigueur by the Sioux, Mandans, Assiniboins, and Blackfeet.

Relieved of her cargo, the *Yellow Stone* felt her way from shallow to shallow. Chouteau, after considering a horseback trip to the fort, decided to stay with his comfortable quarters on board. The final miles to Tecumseh were a mix of vexation and delight for him and the crew. They saw their first antelope and their first herd of buffalo. They discovered that red cedar, almost the only wood they could find, burned tolerably well. A rise in the river finally brought them within sight of the fort, and when they eased the vessel to her landing on 19 June, spring had burst upon the plains and the weather was beautiful.

Fort Tecumseh was almost as great a disappointment to Chouteau, however, as the Ponca post had been. It seemed too squalid to be an entrepôt for the newest mode of river travel. Upon first entering the central quarters, where Laidlaw and his family lived, Chouteau bumped his head on a low beam. Perhaps at that moment, with forehead throbbing and vision momentarily blurred, he made the decision that this outdated little fort must go. Before leaving, he would order a new one built in time for next year's visitation.

A harder decision, made sometime during the eleven days of his visit, was whether or not to try for Fort Union on this trip.

McKenzie, who had recently seen the condition of the river farther upstream, must have joined reluctantly in the conclusion that the *Yellow Stone* must turn around and head downstream. She could try for Fort Union next spring.

It is easy to say that Chouteau ought to have decided on the spot to build another steamboat with a much shallower draft. Instead, he clung to the hope that "improvements" to the *Yellow Stone* would make her more fit for these waters. Actually, the improvements he was to make when he got his craft back to St. Louis were directed toward greater convenience, not more effective navigation. In 1831 there may have been no boatbuilder or marine architect in the country who could have designed a vessel with both a draft shallow enough for the Upper Missouri and ample cargo space, too. That development was years away. So Chouteau had to justify his *Yellow Stone* on other grounds. Was it cheaper to operate than the equivalent tonnage in keelboats? Yes, so long as fuel was free for the taking and if he could keep the vessel working every month of the year. Was it even *possible* to use it in the upper waters? Chouteau and McKenzie must have thought so, for plans already were made for next spring's trip. An earlier start, the experience gained on the present voyage, and a little luck would carry them to Fort Union.

How much faster was the *Yellow Stone* than a keelboat? That depended on whether one took the long or the short view. In open and unobstructed waters, with fires roaring and the cannonading sound of steam bursting from the escapement pipe, the *Yellow Stone* was faster even against a current of six to eight miles an hour. But when delays were averaged with the days of clear sailing, the story was different. In 1804, Lewis and Clark had left St. Louis in mid-May with a keelboat and some smaller craft. The nature of their assignment caused many delays, for they were to make scientific observations, construct maps, and stop to council with the Indians. Considering only delays relevant to their mode of travel — the groundings, the layovers on stormy days, the time taken to repair their equipment — it had required 113 days for Lewis and Clark to reach the future site of Fort Tecumseh. The *Yellow Stone* had made it in 64 days. Much better, of course, but not phenomenal. Worse records were still to be set by future steamboats before the average time dropped noticeably.

On 31 June, the *Yellow Stone* headed back downstream for St. Louis. In the hold was a cargo of deerskins, buffalo robes, beaver pelts, and buffalo tongues. In a tiny pen on the main deck were two buffalo calves that Chouteau was taking home to show his friends and neighbors.

It took far less time to go home, thanks to the swift current. The boat docked in St. Louis on 15 July, and Chouteau triumphantly off-loaded his cargo into the American Fur Company warehouse and prepared to make a couple of runs on the lower river. The *Missouri Intelligencer* at Columbia helpfully noted that low water had thwarted the attempt to reach Fort Union but pointed out that Chouteau's *Yellow Stone* had gone 600 miles farther up the river than any previous steam vessel.

Between the end of July and the first of September, the *Yellow Stone* made two trips, identified in the account books as trips A and B. Profit was small, for the boat was not well known to shippers as a packet (that is, a vessel carrying mail, passengers, and freight for the general public), and competing boats had the regular trade sewed up. There were justifications for the voyages, however, beyond profit. The main mission of trip A was to carry supplies to the company's trading house on the Kansas River, where Chouteau's young brother Frederick had gone into business, and to pick up furs from there. The post was on the south side of the Kansas, about seven miles above present-day Lawrence, and the arrival of the *Yellow Stone* may have been another first for Pierre Chouteau, Jr. Proof that the vessel actually went all the way to Frederick's post is not conclusive; the goods could have been off-loaded at the mouth of the Kansas and taken the rest of the way by keelboat. But Prince Maximilian was to record in his diary, in 1833, that the *Yellow Stone* had once been to the Kansas post.

Evidence in the firm's accounts suggests that both trips took the steamboat entirely across the state of Missouri; trip A to the Kansas, and trip B to Cantonment Leavenworth. The passenger list for trip A shows that a "Lt. Rousseau" — who appears to have been Second Lieutenant Gustave Rousseau, a West Pointer who was taking post with the Sixth Infantry under Major Bennet Riley — paid $20 for two cabin passages. His $20 freight bill would have covered the meager household items of a young army officer and his wife.

Two passages of $5 each were charged to "Genl. Clark." As these were not first-class berths, and as William Clark, superintendent of Indian affairs for the region, appears to have been in St. Louis during all of August, he may have been using Indian Department funds to send a couple of visiting chiefs on their way home. On trip B, someone paid $3 for a "Mountain boy's passage." The several $2 passages were paid by travelers willing to sleep on the decks. On the manifest for trip B appears the entry, "Mormonites fr[eigh]t & Passages 215.00." In 1831 the Mormons or Latter Day Saints had begun to settle in and around Independence, Missouri. Trip A shows a freight bill of $16 to "J. Smith," probably the Mormon leader Joseph Smith, who may have been among the several cabin passengers not listed by name. He and several elders dedicated a temple site at Independence on 8 August, then returned to the church headquarters in Ohio. The "W. Phelps" listed as a passenger on trip A was probably William A. Phelps, moving to Independence to begin publication of the *Evening and Morning Star* and the *Upper-Missouri Advertizer,* both Mormon publications. His press and other printing equipment may have been a part of the cargo.

After trip B came a period of renovation and refurnishing, including a "Cabbin & Hurricane deck" built primarily by the firm of Kennedy & Ferguson. A summary of the $666.41 spent for this work is the only evidence that another section of berths and private quarters was added to the original cabin, and a hurricane deck placed over the entire structure. (A "cabin" contained several compartments and a public room.) Because all the pictorial representations of the *Yellow Stone* were made after this renovation and clearly show the completed cabin and hurricane deck, we have no way of knowing exactly what the vessel looked like before the remodeling.

From Joseph Charless, who had moved to St. Louis in 1808 to start a newspaper and now was a merchant, came materials for painting and decorating. The basic color of the vessel appears to have been white, with yellow trim. Because all paints were mixed on the job by adding various pigments to white lead or linseed oil, the order called for lampblack, bluish-green verdigris (a copper compound), red litharge (a lead compound), yellow ochre, copal and japan varnishes, and, of course, turpentine in large quantities.

The small, miscellaneous accounts in the Chouteau papers show an attempt to transform the *Yellow Stone* from a working boat to one that provided at least minimal amenities for crew and passengers. Thomas Barnett supplied a Franklin stove for $12 and a deck stove for $41.62, with the necessary stovepiping. He also provided an engine lamp with a supply of "oil fat" to burn in it. Other new lighting fixtures included seven glass and three tin lanterns. A gross of curtain rings was ordered, eight chairs added to the cabin, window blinds hung, and $7.50 paid to "Ladies for making Sheets."

A final touch was a huge American flag, measuring twelve by eighteen feet, shown in a Catlin painting (p. xxvi) and an 1832 broadside (p. 72).

By October the refurbishing was complete and the hold was filling with cargo. Now the packs of skins and robes that had been coming down the Missouri from the summer hunts and from the company's posts on the Mississippi went aboard. Each pack was given a number and entered into record books that still survive. A commodity not usually thought of in relation to the Indian trade is lead, which was melted in crude furnaces and shipped downriver, especially from the region around Dubuque, Iowa, and Galena, Illinois, in chunks called "pigs." It was a production mainly of the Sauks, Foxes, and Winnebagoes, although by this time the white settlers were encroaching upon the mines. Several tons went aboard.

When the new captain, Andrew Bennett, yanked the bell rope at departure time, a few of the old crew members were still with the boat, including Postlethwaite, who stayed on as engineer and probably went south with the vessel. Now the *Yellow Stone* was beginning a new line of work, and for the rest of her tenure under American Fur Company control she would ascend the Missouri in the spring and summer, then retire to the warm bayous of the lower Mississippi in winter to transport sugar cane and cotton, while her officers awaited word from St. Louis that the ice was breaking up on the wild Missouri.

2

---◆---

Platform
for an
Artist's Easel

◆IC THE DEPARTURE of the *Yellow Stone* in the spring of 1832 was its most spectacular one, combining some of the glamour of an Atlantic sailing with the frantic hilarity of a Green River rendezvous of mountain men. The oversized flag of the nation rippled from the stern, and the long, triangular banner of the American Fur Company flew from the jackstaff at the bow. It was Fort Union or bust this time.

Chouteau had spent the winter as usual in New York, preparing for this exciting year. The most inviting prospect was not a potential bonanza in furs (everyone complained that trade was dropping off), but the incentive of pushing the *Yellow Stone* farther upstream than last year and enjoying her new and more comfortable living quarters.

In New York, Ramsay Crooks had asked Chouteau to collect some mineral specimens during the voyage. "Limestone, Sandstone, Coal, or other formations you may meet with. Stones and Pebbels of all sorts. Chrystals or any other productions of that kind." For his part, Crooks promised to make a lobbying visit to Washington to see what could be done about getting permission to ship more liquor into the Indian country. The law allowed only enough whisky for the personal use of boat crews and *engagés* to be taken upriver; what the company wanted was a supply for those Indians who came in contact with the Hudson's Bay Company traders, who dispensed whisky freely. Crooks wrote to Chouteau in the spring that he would prefer Canada and the United States agree to ban whisky completely. He asked how much liquor Chouteau thought he would need to counter the generosity of the Hudson's Bay people. "Don't tell me how much you would like to have, but what will really be required for protection, & for that *only*."

The old *Yellow Stone* — she was traveled enough to be called old, with affection — had steam up by midday on 26 March. That was comfortably earlier than the previous year's embarkation, and with luck she could take advantage of both the early spring and June rises. Chouteau had prepared a document listing everyone to be transported on the vessel (reproduced as Appendix B, p. 167). The historian who first encounters this document among the papers of the Chouteau family glows in the belief that he has found a rarity — a passenger list of the *Yellow Stone* for the spring voyage of 1832. The heading says so. And the crew members are listed, along with a number of men who might logically have needed to be on the Upper Missouri for the season.

But traders McKenzie, Laidlaw, and Lamont, and Lucien Fontenelle are listed, too, although we know that McKenzie was at Fort Union, making plans to come down and meet Chouteau somewhere along the river. William Laidlaw, still in charge at Fort Tecumseh, was hurriedly working on the new fort mandated by Chouteau last year. Fontenelle was waiting at Tecumseh for several *engagés* to accompany him on a western expedition. It is difficult to say where Daniel Lamont might have been; he could have been on the steamboat, but the other three definitely were not. So the list is not a manifest of *Yellow Stone* passengers. The key to its purpose is penciled lightly on the back: "General Clark." It was Clark's duty, as superintendent of Indian matters, to issue "passports" to persons going up the

Missouri and to authorize the shipment of enough liquor to sustain such men while they were on the job.

What Chouteau gave the superintendent is basically a full roster of his Upper Missouri men plus the crew of the *Yellow Stone* — and Clark undoubtedly understood full well the inflated nature of the document. We can assume that *most* of the men named on it were aboard. But it was to Chouteau's advantage to list everyone he could, thus increasing the amount of liquor in the permit that Clark would issue him. In this case it was to be 1500 gallons.

The dozens of *engagés,* conveniently lumped together as "boatmen" on the Chouteau list, were mostly aboard. Men did not winter on the Upper Missouri if they could avoid it, but these *voyageurs,* near the bottom of the ladder in frontier society, ranked just above free blacks. Many had Indian blood. As the *engagés* were mostly illiterate, their names may appear garbled as written by an American clerk. Still, a few achieved brief footnotes in history. Chouteau's list includes the name of boatman François Robidoux, usually spoken of as "one of the Robidoux brothers," active in founding the city of St. Joseph and who ranged wide in the fur-trading world. And there is interpreter Baptiste — probably Jean Baptiste — Dorion, whose grandfather had been with Lewis and Clark and whose brother had been massacred in 1813 as one of the Astorians along the Columbia River. Jean Baptiste would himself turn up later as an interpreter for Joseph N. Nicollet and other travelers.

Best known among the boatmen was Henry Chatillon, who would become a guide and hunter for Francis Parkman in the summer of 1846 and be written of as "brave and true-hearted" in Parkman's masterpiece, *Oregon Trail.*

The most interesting travelers aboard the *Yellow Stone,* as she ticked off the few miles of the Mississippi and turned once more into the brown waters of the Missouri, are not on Chouteau's list at all. Together they were the personalities that make the 1832 passenger list both varied and unique.

For one thing, there were women. Some female members of

Chouteau's family, perhaps with a few friends, were riding as far as St. Charles and would return the next day by carriage. They may have included Chouteau's wife, Emilie Anne, or his daughters Julia and Emilie. There was as yet no ladies' cabin on the vessel, but no doubt special compartments had been set aside for their temporary use. The other non-employees were as mixed as any storyteller could wish for. There was George Catlin, lawyer turned artist, who had come west with an unquenchable desire to paint Indians and western scenes, and was traveling as a guest of the company. And John F. A. Sanford, the young fiancé of Emilie Chouteau and subagent to the Mandans, returning to his summer home with the tribe. He also supervised the Gros Ventres, Crows, Arikaras, Assiniboins, and the Knisteneau tribe. Four Indians from Sanford's group were aboard, returning from Washington, where they had been guests of the government.

Another passenger was Joshua Pilcher, a fur trader turned subagent, who had been to Washington with Sanford and his wards and who would in a few brief years replace William Clark as superintendent in St. Louis.

Finally, there were two Nez Perce Indians who had come an incredible distance, journeying down the river in search of what many of their white Christian brothers thought was redemption: the Holy Spirit. Whatever their quest, they already had become a legend, and American missionaries were soon to follow them home as the westward movement gained momentum.

---◈---

The two young Nez Perces were all that remained of four who had left their village near the present Idaho-Montana boundary almost a year earlier, on a mission that American religious zeal and cultural cross-purposes would turn into a Christian pilgrimage. Joining a trading party led by Lucien Fontenelle and Andrew Drips, they had reached St. Louis in the fall of 1831, looking for William Clark. Not only was he their Great Father, but many older persons among the Nez Perce still had pleasant memories of the Lewis and Clark Expedition twenty-five years earlier. They knew Clark to be a compassionate and understanding man.

What the men said to Clark, and what happened then, is obscured by the dust of years and the sketchiness of the written record. They seem to have told Clark that a couple of their young tribesmen had returned from Canada, claiming the white man had a book that told him how to conduct himself and that was filled with the power of the Great Spirit. They were not necessarily seeking the book to substitute for their own religious beliefs and icons, but to augment and supplement them. More power, stronger medicine, more of whatever knowledge the white man had that seemed to bring so many good things to him.

Originally the men had included three Nez Perces and a Flathead. In St. Louis they all were called Flatheads, and were welcomed by Clark and certain church leaders. In all the thousands of pages of correspondence left from Clark's years as superintendent of Indian affairs, there is not a line about these four men and their mission. Therefore, not a word to tell us how Clark viewed their quest, or whether he did anything for them that he would not have done for any other Indian.

During their stay in St. Louis two of the men died, presumably of ailments of the white man for which their bodies were unprepared. Those who died included a Nez Perce warrior from the Kamiah Valley, whose English name was Eagle, and Man of the Morning, from the Clearwater River, whose mother was a Flathead.

Now the *Yellow Stone* was carrying the remaining pair back toward their homeland. They were about twenty years of age, one called Rabbit Skin Leggins and the other, No Horns on His Head. The throbbing decks of the steamboat could not have seemed strange to them by now, for they had spent a sabbatical of numbingly new experiences in St. Louis. What must have puzzled them, as they stood watching fireman John or Richmond heaving chunks of wood into the fireboxes, or sat on the hurricane deck and observed the care with which pilot La Barge was nosing the bow through snags and between sandbars, was the question of whether they had failed or succeeded in their mission. Each carried Bibles, rosaries, and other religious artifacts given them by their benefactors. Was there any magic in them for an Indian? They had not failed; they left behind them in St. Louis a smoldering fire, like sparks from a flint that lay glowing red in a handful of aspen shavings.

William Walker, of Ohio, had been in St. Louis in the fall of 1831 and claimed to have visited the four Indians, although he incorrectly described them as having tapered heads. Now this image of the men from beyond the Bitterroots began to gestate in Walker's mind, and during the coming winter he would write to G. P. Disoway, a Methodist acquaintance in New York, about his experience. Disoway, a layman who was a strong supporter of missionary work, would send Walker's letter to the editor of the *Christian Advocate and Journal and Zion's Herald,* adding his own endorsement:

How deeply touching is the circumstance of the four natives traveling on foot 3,000 miles through thick forests and extensive prairies, sincere searchers after truth! The story had scarcely a parallel in history. . . . With what intense concern will men of God whose souls are fired with holy zeal for the salvation of their fellow beings, read their history! . . . May we not indulge the hope that the day is not far distant when the missionaries will penetrate into these wilds where the Sabbath bell has never tolled since the world began!

Upon reading this cry, missionaries would soon be girding up to head west, not to the villages of the two Nez Perces but at least to their corner of the world. The Methodists would send the Rev. Jason Lee on a mission to the Flatheads in 1833, nosing out the Presbyterians and Congregationalists only by an accident of scheduling. Dr. Marcus Whitman would tour the Pacific Northwest in 1835, and return the next year with his wife Narcissa (the first white woman to cross the Rockies) to establish a mission to the Cayuse tribe at Walla Walla.

Rabbit Skin Leggins and No Horns on His Head, who had journeyed far from the Northwest seeking "the white man's book."

Neither Rabbit Skin Leggins nor No Horns on His Head would learn of their eventual success, for No Horns would die near the mouth of the Yellowstone and his companion would be killed by Blackfeet soon after his return home. Another kind of fame lay ahead, however, for artist Catlin had his eye on them, and a blank canvas was waiting as the *Yellow Stone* bellowed along.

———◆———

On a later voyage aboard a company steamboat, John James Audubon would complain that the decks shuddered so constantly and the engine roared so deafeningly that sketching was almost impossible. Perhaps Catlin worked only when the *Yellow Stone* had shut down for the day, or when it was aground or visiting one of the posts. A few of his sketches appear to have been made from the deck, however, and he was so impatient that he probably accomplished what he could while under way.

Born in Wilkes-Barre, Pennsylvania, in 1796, Catlin had studied and practiced law before his love of the outdoors overcame him. He called himself a "Nimrodical lawyer" who would rather fish than prepare briefs. Finally, selling his law library and all his possessions except his rifle and fishing tackle, he went off to Philadelphia to commence painting without a teacher. His obsession with Indians saved him from a life as a so-so painter of portraits in the city. His life changed the day a party of western Indians came through Philadelphia. Catlin saw them "wrapped in their pictured robes, with their brows plumed with the quills of the war-eagle," and he was lost forever. He went to St. Louis in 1830, traveled with William Clark to the Upper Mississippi, and ascended the Missouri as far north as the Platte.

To Catlin, the *Yellow Stone* was just another steamboat, a means of getting an eager man to places where he wanted to work. His journals, which later became letters to the *New York Commercial Advertiser* and then a two-volume compilation of text and engravings, tell us little about the time he was to spend on board. "We tugged, and puffed, and blowed, and toiled for three months," he wrote, and for him that was enough to say about a steamboat.

Catlin's two obsessions were Indians as people and Indians as models for his sketch pad and easel. Not an exploiter of native peoples, he must have entertained disturbing thoughts about the traders whose guest he was. Years later he wrote a passage that showed his feelings for the men and women he freely called savages in the manner of that time:

I love a people who have always made me welcome to the best they had . . . who are honest without laws, who have no jails and no poor-house . . . who never take the name of God in vain . . . who worship God without a Bible, and I believe that God loves them also . . . who are free from religious animosities . . . who have never raised a hand against me, or stolen my property, where there was no law to punish either . . . and oh! how I love a people who don't live for the love of money.

Critics have always had a problem with Catlin. He was a hasty and often imprecise painter; Karl Bodmer, who was to follow him up the river the following year, was far superior. As a keeper of diaries, Catlin's work fell short of being documentary. In his rush to tell the world what he was seeing, he was often inaccurate in details. He reported that the *Yellow Stone* was hauling a twelve-pounder cannon to Fort Union, which was untrue and illogical. A six-pounder might have been part of the freight, but it was unlikely to have been used in firing salutes from the deck as Catlin claimed. The half hour of "continuous cannonading" that he reports hearing as the *Yellow Stone* approached Fort Pierre was probably a series of shots from the much smaller signal cannon thought to have been aboard. Perhaps to a man who would be deaf by the age of fifty-five, all artillery fire sounded about the same.

It is easier to appreciate Catlin's contribution to western ethnography and history if we think of him not primarily as an artist but as a pictorial journalist. Were he alive today, we might expect to find him festooned with cameras and carrying a tape

In 1849, William Fisk portrayed George Catlin surrounded by
works that had made him famous as an Indian artist.

recorder, slogging through some exotic rain forest on assignment for the *National Geographic*. Historian and anthropologist John C. Ewers has said of him, "To accomplish so much in a single summer Catlin had to work very quickly. Many of his paintings of Indians were impressionistic — omitting or merely approximating the details of his sitters' costumes or of Indian actions in their villages, in their camp movements, or on their hunts or war expeditions."

After a brief stop at Cabanné's, the *Yellow Stone* entered a reach of the river that presented a calmer scene to Catlin, who had called the lower river "a huge deformity of waters." "There is," he said, "a terror in its manner which is sensibly felt . . . scarcely an eddy or resting-place for a canoe." The first spring rise had come and gone, and the June rise — brought by melting snows far away in the mountains — was still to come. In seafaring terms, the steamboat was becalmed.

The crew got clear of an area that had plagued them the year before at Ponca Creek, but struck impossibly low water below the mouth of White River a thousand miles from St. Louis. With apprehension growing at Fort Tecumseh, as it had the year before, Laidlaw sent three men down in a skiff to look for Chouteau. One reason for the impatience was a repeat of last year's dilemma: Lucien Fontenelle was waiting at the fort with twenty men and needed another twenty from the *Yellow Stone* before he could take off for the mountains. Also, McKenzie, thinking the steamboat might fail again to reach his post, had come down from Fort Union with a great cargo of beaver and had been waiting a month.

Again, Chouteau decided to send a party overland to advise Laidlaw of his plight and perhaps get a couple of keelboats to come down and take off some of the cargo. Eighteen men reached the fort on 18 May, Catlin among them. He said it took the steamboat "several weeks" to catch up with them at the fort. Actually she arrived on 31 May, making the time just under two weeks.

A set of raw, new buildings awaited the travelers, a great improvement over the wretched structures that Chouteau had found last year. With many a wine glass raised in the headquarters rooms and many a canteenful of whisky drunk by crew and *engagés*, the place was christened Fort Pierre Chouteau, later shortened to Fort Pierre.

The new fort was built just upriver from the old one, on the right bank near the mouth of the Bad River, now the site of Pierre, South Dakota. When complete it would include a stockade of cottonwood logs, about 300 feet square with blockhouses at two corners. Inside the hollow square, paralleling the walls of the stockade, would be the living quarters, shops, and warehouses.

While he waited for the *Yellow Stone* to arrive, Catlin painted constantly. Hundreds of Sioux had come in to trade upon learning that the steamboat was on the way, and every one was a candidate for a Catlin portrait. He painted Rabbit Skin Leggins again, having made one likeness of him at St. Louis. Among other notables whose portraits found their way into the Catlin gallery were One Horn, a principal Sioux chief, and Black Rock and Tobacco. Soon most of the Sioux bands were represented, and there was a general clamor from those who had not yet been invited to pose. "The vanity of these men, after they had agreed to be painted, was beyond description," Catlin wrote. He painted women and children, and scenes of Indian life, and wrote happily to the *Advertiser* of his experiences.

Later he would tell Chouteau that old General Pratte had feared the letters describing the Upper Missouri "might excite the public attention to something like competition in the Fur trade, by inducing others to undertake in opposition to the American Fur Company." The old refrain.

Though Catlin's paintings would outlive his effusive commentary on Indian life, they were not going to please every artist who later came this way. "Ah! Mr. Catlin," wrote Audubon after his voyage up the Missouri in 1843, "I am now sorry to see and to read your accounts of the Indians *you* saw — how very different they must have been from any that I have seen!" But there is a kind of irony here, since Audubon was producing paintings of birds that some artists and birdwatchers thought were overdramatized, more birdlike than the real thing.

———◊———

Using the name Fort Pierre for the first time in a letter to the company office in St. Louis, Laidlaw wrote that the *Yellow Stone* had pulled out for Fort Union on 5 June with Chouteau in good spirits. Even a day's steaming upriver now would set a record, giving him new prestige among the tribes that already were awed by the steamboat, and renewing the *esprit* of the officials and employees of the company. Nobody on board would have been content, however, with a barely broken record. They had to reach Fort Union this time. The four Indians who were traveling with agent Sanford came back on board when the *Yellow Stone* left Fort Pierre, proceeding home, but with their saga still incomplete. It had not been their idea to go to Washington. They had got caught up in the current notion that bringing Indians east in small groups was good policy. Perhaps this time the plan had originated with Lewis Cass, the secretary of war and national guardian of all the Indians under American influence. More likely, it was conceived by Sanford himself. He was not at home in the wilds, writing frequently to William Clark with complaints about the stingy government that shorted him on supplies and interpreters. And there was Emilie Chouteau, his betrothed, always waiting for him in St. Louis.

He had asked for extra expense money in advance to cover assembling and bringing in men from the various tribes, saying that the task would be arduous, hazardous, and costly. Clark advised Cass, who agreed that Sanford should come on. So the agent headed off to the outer fringes of his district to collect a band of sojourners. They lived so far away that Fort Union would have seemed "back east," and several of the adventurous men from the Ojibway, Assiniboin, and Sioux tribes turned back before reaching St. Louis. The rest arrived by mackinaw boat in

November 1831, and the lionizing began. Catlin was there, painting away.

The Great Father's world was unbelievable. For a while, as their boat entered the settled area on the lower reaches of the Missouri, the Indians had tried to keep a count of the houses by cutting notches in a pipestem, and when the stem gave out they switched to a long stick. The sticks multiplied. Finally, as they came in sight of St. Louis with its 15,000 citizens, the carefully kept record was tossed overboard. The object lesson the government wanted to teach them — that the whites were as numerous as the leaves of the forest — was learned early.

Sanford relished the bright lamps and heady enjoyments of St. Louis for a while, then got his tour on the road to Washington. Because he had waited until January to start, water travel was impossible and the party moved by stagecoach. Two French interpreters, who had probably come down from Sanford's agency, augmented the group, as well as Joshua Pilcher, who would spend his time in Washington lobbying to get the job held by John Dougherty, subagent at Fort Leavenworth. Pilcher would claim that Dougherty had been at that post for five years without visiting the tribes under his control. Pilcher would fail to get Dougherty's job, but Dougherty would be ordered to move up to Bellevue, where he could be closer to his tribes.

Although this kind of colorful Indian troupe had been barnstorming through white settlements and eastern cities for at least forty years, it never failed to attract a crowd and a reporter from the local paper. The Frederick, Maryland, *Herald* explained that the Indians "reside in remote sections of our territory in the vicinity of the Rocky Mountains, and are entire strangers to the arts of civilization." But they were fast learners and had spent a month and a half in civilized St. Louis before starting eastward.

On they went, along a well-traveled route for tours of this nature, to Baltimore and then Washington (the famous Brown's Hotel), and word was spreading among government officials that Sanford was a high-priced tour guide. In mid-January he submitted an itemized account of what he had spent thus far for the pay of interpreters, boatmen, and ferrymen; stage and train fares; rations and clothing for the Indians; and medical bills, including a charge for smallpox vaccination. It amounted to about $2400. Then Sanford estimated what it would cost to get these people back home. More travel and rations, wages and presents. Another $4000. The estimate for presents alone was $1000. There was outrage in Congress and some paper-shuffling among the small staff at the War Department, but in the end the taxpayers came up with most of the money.

The charge that Congress criticized most was the extra pay that Sanford wanted for the risk and trouble of going off into the wilder edges of his district to bring the delegation in. General William H. Ashley, making his first speech on the floor of the House as a representative from Missouri, concluded that Sanford was paid to do that sort of thing and should receive nothing extra. Ashley, who claimed to be well acquainted with the country the delegation had come from, maintained that no real hardship had been encountered. Perhaps the real problem was Sanford himself — later to become known as the owner of the slave Dred Scott — always a "summertime" agent who preferred to spend his time in St. Louis. As historian Dale Morgan has said, "His was a most glaring case of the exploitation of the Indian service in the interest of the American Fur Company."

Of the four Indians who had by this time seen just about all there was of American civilization, two are nameless and unknown. The third was Broken Arm, a Yanktonnais Sioux. But the exploits of the fourth made the best story. His name, freely translated, was the Light, although Catlin got it wrong and called him the Pigeon's Egg Head, a name that still turns up in history books. His Indian name, also from Catlin, was Wi-jun-jon.

The Light was one of those persons who, coming from whatever rural barnyard or far-off arctic tundra, could accept the urban life without hesitation and embrace it gladly. He was a

Catlin's canvas depicts the Light in the dignity of his Indian
dress and as a foppish "tame" Indian.

natural *bon vivant*. Certainly he filled two of the requirements for that designation: He came from a good family, being the first son of Iron Arrow Point, chief of the Stone Band of the Assiniboins; and he was striking in appearance. Standing tall, the strong cheekbones and bronze skin of the Indian accentuated; nose a bit Roman, chin stronger than most, hair shining like long threads of black volcanic glass. He loved to dress well, and no matter how taken he might be with European garb — those silly beaver hats, tapered trousers, and colored weskits — he knew what drew the eyes of the Americans. He stuck to soft buckskins, spectacular mountain-goat mantles, and elaborate decorations made of porcupine quills.

He stuck with them, that is, until his group arrived at the White House and visited with President Andrew Jackson. The President gave the Light a general's uniform — more about that later.

He postured, drew admiring looks from fashionable ladies, and waved at crowds. Another famed painter of Indians, Charles Bird King, got him to pose and entitled the portrait "Assiniboin Indian from the Most Remote Tribe that Had Ever Visited Washington Previous to 1838."

At last the Grand Tour was over. The Light and his fellows headed back for the country where whites who knew no better could call you "just another Indian," even if your father was Iron Arrow Point. Sanford had arranged passage on the *Yellow Stone* and the voyage soon would end. Where does an Indian eat aboard a steamboat if he has recently been housed at Brown's Hotel and smoked a pipe with the President? Does he dine with Chouteau and Captain Bennett, using the boat's best china? Or does he sit crosslegged in the crew's quarters, getting used to coarse fare in the knowledge that he soon will be dipping his fingers into a communal pot in an Assiniboin lodge?

Catlin tells the rest of the Light's story, and his account is confirmed in the journals of trader Edwin T. Denig and referred to by trader Charles Larpenteur, both reliable observers. The Light's village was below Fort Union. When he swaggered down the gangplank at the landing, he was wearing his military finery. That meant a general's rumpled uniform, its blue piping soiled, its epaulets tangled and tarnished. A broadsword dangled at his side. The plume on his hat drooped like the tail of a despondent peacock. He carried a broken fan and an umbrella with bent ribs, and under his arm was a keg of whisky. Around his neck, suspended by a twisted ribbon, was the medal traditionally given to prominent visiting Indians by the President.

For a while the Light was the talk of the village, but with each story he told at the campfire, skepticism grew. Before long, some of his tribesmen were calling him a liar. In the months that followed, a particularly damaging legend sprang up around the Light (perhaps even nurtured by him), that the magic, the medicine instilled in him, made him impervious to leaden bullets. One night, after a session during which the Light's stories had seemed unusually irksome, a tribesman filed a piece of iron down to the size of a lead ball, in case ordinary lead was the key to the magic, and loaded a musket with it. Firing through the tipi, where the Light's shadow was sharpened by the brilliant firelight, the assailant killed him.

Far to the west, the Light's traveling companion Broken Arm fared better. He was destined to become an important chief of the Crees, a tribal delegate to treaties at Fort Laramie and elsewhere. At an 1855 council on the Missouri, at the mouth of a river that William Clark had named the Judith in honor of his sweetheart, Broken Arm represented the Crees at the first treaty between the United States and the various related Cree and Blackfoot tribes. It is not likely that in any of the gear he brought home from Washington was there an umbrella, a top hat, or the dream of a life he never could have.

———————◆———————

When the *Yellow Stone* left Fort Pierre to make its second attempt to reach Fort Union, the pilot could sense one great difference in the way the craft handled. It rode higher, because the deckhands had been unloading summer supplies at all the stops. Most of the *engagés* had dropped off, too, with their gear.

On the other hand, the river was falling daily. The June rise had moved downstream. There would be more occasions to send out the yawl for soundings, to ram the vessel across bars by sheer steam power, or to use the spars. Sparring meant rigging two straight and tough logs of peeled yellow pine so that, with the winding action of the capstan, they could "walk" the vessel across a sandbar.

The shores of the Missouri this far upstream were barren. There were buffalo to kill, but there was not enough wood to burn. There were old, abandoned trading posts but few active ones. The *Yellow Stone* passed one wood area called the "navy yard," where keelboats and pirogues were made by carpenters from Fort Pierre. Then came the mouth of the Cheyenne, a river flowing in from the mountains; and, in a single day, there were four more streams — the Little Cheyenne, Moreau, Grand, and Rampart rivers.

The Mandan villages were a major stopover between Pierre and Fort Union. They were the site of the company's year-old post, Fort Clark, where trader James Kipp was in charge. Sanford's quarters were near here, and no doubt he went ashore with no enthusiasm. Already he had received permission to spend the next winter in St. Louis. The Mandans were a light-skinned people, comparatively speaking, whom Catlin and many scholars of that day thought were descended from a lost expedition of Welshmen. They had befriended Lewis and Clark, who had spent the entire winter of 1804–1805 with them and, unlike the irritable Arikaras, the Mandans managed not to show their dismay at the inroads of white America. They were, in the parlance of many Caucasians, "good" Indians, but the traders and agents who were to deal more intimately with them found them less admirable, perhaps even rascally.

Their gastronomic customs fascinated Catlin. One dish was made from rotting buffalo carcasses, the riper the better. The Mandans buried whole animals in the fall for disinterment in the spring, and Catlin reported that while the stench was intolerable the soup was considered delicious. He did not claim to have tried it.

Here George Watson, the first engineer, got caught up in trading fever and disposed of some articles in exchange for beaver skins and buffalo robes. He would hear about that later when Jacob Halsey, of Fort Clark, reported him to the St. Louis office. Watson's job was to keep the engine cylinder packed with hemp and the bearings well lubricated, and not to muscle in on the fur business.

Now the final stop, Fort Union, was just upriver from the mouth of the Yellowstone — a kind of landmark, like the Platte, for travelers since before Lewis and Clark. Not far away was an elevation called McKenzie's Butte, where the Scotsman would in later years stand and watch for the company steamboat. He said he could see the smoke from the chimneys a day before the boat arrived, because of its slow rate of speed in the twisting channel.

In describing the arrival of the *Yellow Stone* Catlin, with his usual tendency to exaggerate, reported that the Indians threw themselves on their faces, or shot their horses and dogs to appease whatever gods of smoke and thunder had brought this monster to them. He was fascinated by the conviction that their buffalo herds were doomed. A few days before his arrival at Fort Union, he wrote, an immense herd had appeared across the river. A party of 500 to 600 Indians on horseback had forded the river, returning with 1400 fresh buffalo tongues for sale to McKenzie. They wanted whisky in exchange.

Catlin would now move west to visit more distant tribes and return down the river with a couple of French boatmen. As for McKenzie, he was preparing an outfit to go up the Yellowstone to the mouth of the Big Horn, hoping to establish trade with the Crows and other mountain tribes.

The fort was the usual quadrangle, surrounded by a stockade and with blockhouses at two corners. It would not have been

Fort Union, with the butte in the foreground from which Kenneth McKenzie used to watch for smoke from approaching steamboats.

an unusual structure back east on the Ohio or Mississippi, but its location in this wild place made it seem totally foreign. It lay on an alluvial height on the north bank of the Missouri, the river flowing only sixty feet from the front gate. Behind the fort, the prairie led back to a chain of hills; there was a patch of woods on the opposite shore. Inside the hollow square, McKenzie's one-story house, built of cottonwood, featured eight glass windows. The other buildings were conventional, functional.

No field crops or vegetables were raised here, for the growing season was too short. But hogs and milk cows foraged nearby or were confined in pens near the post.

McKenzie's life was filled with anachronisms and ironies. He not only set a comparatively lavish table in a land that provided little but meat and enjoyed his glass windows in a land of Indian huts and tipis; he also used utterly disparate modes of transportation for his goods. Even as the *Yellow Stone* rested at the landing with cold boilers, McKenzie was dispatching teams of pack dogs to haul loads overland. These were not merely sled dogs, used in the Eskimo fashion, but real pack dogs. They provided a traditional mode of travel for the Indians of the High Plains, recalling the days before these tribes had obtained horses. McKenzie would complain to James Kipp in late 1833 that he had failed to get enough dogs from the Assiniboins, and would ask Kipp to send him a few teams — he called them "trains" — of good dogs.

Chouteau wasted little time at Fort Union because the river was falling. After celebrating one more victory over the Opposition, after taking on hundreds of packs of robes and skins, the *Yellow Stone* backed away from the muddy landing and took the current. It was the middle of June, and by early July the vessel was home in St. Louis and the world was learning of her achievement. If General Pratte really feared that Catlin might be talking too much about the high country, he must have grimaced now as the letters and newspaper clippings began to arrive.

The *Missouri Republican* wrote a column that would be copied soon by other editors:

This enterprise will no doubt greatly add to our trade and intercourse with the Indians, and subtract from that of the British trader. There is nothing, we are sure, that could have excited a greater degree of surprise among the wild inhabitants of the upper Missouri, than the appearance among them of a high pressure steamboat, moving majestically against the current. . . . Many of the Indians, who had been in the habit of trading with the Hudson Bay Company, declared that the company could no more compete with the Americans, and concluded hereafter to bring all their skins to the latter. . . . We are informed by Captain B[ennett] that thousands of the natives visited the boat, were very friendly, and invited him to several feasts prepared in honor of the occasion.

From France came a note from old J. J. Astor, attesting that the voyage had attracted much attention in Europe. He even wrote again, asking Chouteau for more details of the trip. Ramsay Crooks wrote from New York to send congratulations, but his real accolade was to come later that fall when the implications of the achievement had become more clear and he declared, "The future history of the Mo. will preserve for you the honorable and enviable distinction of having accomplished an object of immense importance, by exhibiting the practicality of conquering the obstructions of the Missouri, considered till almost the present day insurmountable to Steamboats."

In fact, the river was still all but insurmountable. That notion had bothered Chouteau the year before, in the shallows near the Ponca post, and this year when he was delayed for so long below the White River. Something was wrong with this plucky steamboat. She needed a shallower draft, greater power, larger wheels — *something*.

3

The Deadly Cargoes

◄C I N T H E S P R I N G A N D S U M M E R of 1832, the Congress took two steps to better the lives of those Indians considered to be under United States protection and control. In both instances the mandate of Congress was humane, practical, and promised early benefits. In both cases the will of the lawmakers was thwarted by the venality of certain frontier tradesmen or obeyed incompletely and carelessly by Washington bureaucrats. In both cases the *Yellow Stone* was involved.

Most Americans agreed that liquor was bad for the Indians. They should not be allowed to have it unless circumstances made it necessary, or at least expedient, as when a trader was bargaining for a season's harvest of deerskins or a negotiator was persuading a tribal chief to put his X on a treaty. In such cases a gill or two of whisky often seemed the only sensible inducement.

Officially, the policy of the government was unyielding, at least on the statute books. The early colonists had placed restrictions on the use of rum in the Indian trade, but these were not effective. Neither were the measures enacted for control of liquor in the old Northwest Territory. When Jefferson had urged Congress to pass a federal law, it had authorized him, in the Trade and Intercourse Act of 1802, to take such measures "as to him may appear expedient to prevent or restrain the vending or distributing of spirituous liquors among all or any of the said Indian tribes." Letters went out, forbidding liquor traffic, but to little avail.

An amendment to the law of 1802 was added on 6 May 1822, authorizing the President to direct the searching of all traders' goods by agents, territorial governors, or military officers; the forfeit of any liquor found; and the lifting of the license of the offending trader. There were loopholes and much resistance from the fur industry, but the amendment did enable Major General Edmund P. Gaines, commanding the Western Department of the Army, to send a memorandum to all his post commanders, enclosing a copy of the new regulation and ordering the officers to inspect the stores of all traders if there was a suspicion of violation. Any liquor found was to be confiscated and the trader brought to court. The loophole here was the word *suspicion,* a subjective term. No suspicion, no search.

Although the provision was not watertight, it was bothersome to Astor and his associates, who by January 1828 had found a way around it. The War Department was persuaded to issue a letter to agents and territorial governors that authorized them to issue permits for the taking of limited quantities of whisky into Indian country to be used only by the traders and their employees. Quantity was limited to a gill a day per man, and the liquor was never to be used in trade or barter — or given to the Indians.

For a while, Astor and his staff thought that they could live with the new ruling. A little carelessness by inspectors, and perhaps some padding of employee rolls to increase the allotment — it might work out.

The American Fur Company felt it had a better reason than other traders to keep a bit of liquor on hand for the Indians, considering how freely it was dispensed by Canadian traders. That was a strong lobbying position for Ramsay Crooks when he went to Washington. There is little doubt that the Hudson's Bay Company had an obvious advantage, and Crooks dwelt upon his dilemma as he cajoled the congressmen: although he was himself a strong believer in total prohibition of liquor in Indian country, he was hard pressed to compete with those whisky-peddling Canadians.

In private, around the Astor table, there was talk of other reasons why the concessions already made by the government were not enough. The Opposition in this country was getting its liquor past the inspectors. "Our opponents are well supplied at all their trading posts with Alcohol & wines highly charged with Spirit," ran one letter from McKenzie to William B. Astor.

Again the War Department listened to reason. By 15 June 1831 it had sent out another letter, permitting the American Fur Company to take to each of its posts two barrels of whisky for Indian use. To combat the nefarious Canadian traders, the letter implied, but in the field it was interpreted as applying to all traders, not just to the company in closest competition with the Canadians.

When the *Yellow Stone* embarked in the spring of 1832, Chouteau and his crew had a fairly clear view of what the law and subsequent rulings from Washington allowed them to do. By the act of 1802 and the 1822 amendment they were generally barred from distribution of liquor to the Indians with whom they traded. The exceptions were that they could carry with them a gill a day per man for their employees (the 1828 concession) and two barrels per season to use in the Indian trade (the 1831 concession).

But while Chouteau was establishing his record by steaming to Fort Union, an occurrence in Washington brought the company and all connected with it into a period of turmoil.

———◆———

There is a pattern in American lawmaking that everyone recognizes. An act of Congress is passed and appears to be watertight. Then a few loopholes appear, and some rulings in the various departments of government bite deeper into the usefulness of the law. Enforcement lags. Finally, the need to begin again is obvious, and a congressional committee sends down a new bill intended to tidy up the situation and implement the intent of the old law.

This process had been at work for some months in the matter of liquor for the Indians. Apparently a decision had been made in the War Department, particularly in its Bureau of Indian Affairs headed by Elbert Herring, that the liquor trade was again out of hand. Herring wrote to Superintendent Clark late in 1831 for comments, and probably sent a similar letter to other officials on the frontier. Telling Clark he had heard that licenses to take whisky into the Indian country were being abused, Herring suggested the prospect of complete prohibition. Or, if not complete prohibition then a reduction in the amount of liquor permitted to traders.

Clark's reply gave Herring and his superior, Secretary Lewis Cass, some valuable information that they could take to Congress. Clark wrote that "a more pernicious article could not be introduced among [the Indians]." He quoted Joshua Pilcher, who said he had seen an Omaha chief, Big Elk, carrying an eight-gallon keg of whisky from a trader's house to his lodge. The traders, Clark said, were obviously abusing their privilege. Instead of carrying whisky for their employees, they were taking straight alcohol to be diluted with water later for the Indians. Clark recommended total prohibition as soon as possible. Herring reassured him on 13 January 1832, acknowledging that the abuse of trading licenses was "unconscionable." He added, "Possibly a remedy may be provided before long."

On 9 July 1832 Congress passed "An Act to provide for the appointment of a commissioner of Indian Affairs, and for other purposes." Primarily it recognized the need to give more clout to the bureau or "Indian office" that had been operating as part of the War Department. The new commissioner, Elbert Herring, was to have "the direction and management of all Indian affairs, and of all matters arising out of Indian relations," at a salary of three thousand dollars a year.

Then came Section 4 of the Act: "And be it further enacted, that no ardent spirits shall be hereafter introduced, under any pretence, into the Indian country." There was no equivocation here, no passing of the responsibility back to the President or giving army officers the option of searching or not searching.

Undoubtedly in the halls of Congress there was some young freshman senator naive enough to tell himself: "That takes care of the Indian liquor problem once and for all."

———◈———

Once William Clark and his exploring partner, Meriwether Lewis, had been the two most talked-about men in America. They had taken a small band of soldiers up the Missouri, across the Rockies, and down the Columbia River, bringing them back safely after a winter on the Pacific Coast. Among their tangible rewards were government appointments, Lewis becoming governor of Upper Louisiana and Clark being named superintendent of Indian Affairs for all but one of the western tribes along the Missouri and Mississippi.

Lewis had died early, almost certainly a suicide, and the cares of office may have helped to kill him. Clark had held on in the tumult and intrigue of the frontier, doubling as a brigadier general of militia, and had built a reputation among the Indians and whites for fairness and good will but also for tough-mindedness when necessary. He had served as governor of the new Missouri Territory from 1813 to 1821. Usually, when a territory became a state the supervision of Indians and their agents passed back to the War Department or to the new governor or the governor of a neighboring state. For Clark an exception had been made, and he was retained in 1822 as superintendent at St. Louis.

Now in 1832 he was becoming more of a figurehead — not to the Indians, who still respected him, but to the traders and merchants who had watched him grow old and lax in office. John

Treat Irving saw him in 1833 and wrote, "The General was a fine, soldierlike-looking man, tall and thin. His hair was white; but he seemed to be as hardy and vigorous as ever." But Joshua Pilcher said that Clark's "infirmities and goodness of heart induced an implicite reliance upon everything recommended by his subordinates." After Clark's death, Missouri Senator Benton would declare that his office had become nearly useless in recent years.

Clark had become more and more reliant upon his chief clerk, George Maguire, and more trusting of the traders who brought in their applications for liquor permits. He had begun to let details slide past him. Perhaps this man who had negotiated thirty-seven Indian treaties as evenhandedly as anyone could have was better at dealing with Indians than with his fellow Americans.

At this time his worst problem lay with the tribes of the Upper Mississippi Valley, where a long-standing feud between whites and the confederated Sauk and Fox tribes had finally broken out into what history was prepared to label a war — the Black Hawk War. Resentment and misunderstandings had been troublesome ever since the Sauks and Foxes had sold enormous tracts of land in Illinois, Wisconsin, and Missouri to the government. During the War of 1812, a band of Sauks sympathetic to the British had become so bothersome that Clark had been called upon to go to work in both of his capacities. As superintendent he had tried to negotiate and mitigate; as head of the territorial militia he had sent gunboats up the Mississippi to help keep the peace.

Left over from the British band was a war chief of the Sauks, a gaunt old man named Black Hawk. In April 1832 he had led several hundred men, women, and children eastward across the Mississippi (at Rock Island, Illinois), to their ancestral lands, which they had been made to abandon during the past few years. Black Hawk said they were only going to plant corn in their old fields, but his actions were clearly in violation of at least two treaties and were infuriating to the whites who already had moved onto the land.

At first the Illinois militia had tried to handle the matter, but before long a large detachment of United States regulars was involved. Some had gone to the disputed area from Jefferson Barracks at St. Louis. Others, under General Winfield Scott, had come from the East by way of the Great Lakes. A cholera outbreak had decimated Scott's troops, but after a chase that led into northern Illinois, southern Wisconsin Territory, and west to the Mississippi River, the "war" ended suddenly in the late summer. Overtaken at the Bad Axe River, which enters the Mississippi in southwestern Wisconsin Territory, Black Hawk's band of starving families was fired upon with considerable loss of life. Black Hawk was later captured and held prisoner for a few months, during which time he was escorted to the East Coast to confer with President Jackson.

In August, Clark had embarked on the steamboat *Warrior*, heading for Prairie du Chien in Wisconsin Territory on agency business. Finding cholera aboard, he had decided to transfer to another steamboat at Fort Armstrong, near Rock Island, and return home. Had he continued upriver he would have been an observer at the Battle of Bad Axe, but it is doubtful that Clark's presence would have affected the actions of the steamboat crew and the vengeful troops.

———◆———

Before the *Yellow Stone* embarked on her second voyage of the year on 24 July 1832, Chouteau knew that a stiffer liquor law was making its way through the committees of Congress. William B. Astor had written him about it at least once, on 24 April: "The subject is one involving very materially the interest, if not the existence of our new Posts above the Mandans." He suggested that Chouteau ought to approach General Ashley on a personal basis and encourage General Pratte to do the same. This letter arrived in St. Louis after Chouteau had departed on the year's first voyage, but could have been forwarded by keelboat, as was often done. It is impossible to say when Chouteau learned of the actual passing of the 9 July law. Official word did not reach Clark until 11 September, according to the acknowledgment he sent the War Department.

Still preoccupied with the aftermath of the Black Hawk incident, and no doubt leaving the details of office to his chief clerk, Clark issued the usual permit to Chouteau on the day the *Yellow Stone* sailed. The permit allowed for the transport of 1073 gallons of liquor, enough to sustain about a hundred men for a year at the allotted ration. It is likely that Chouteau, whether or not he knew for certain about the new law, planned a fast turnaround when the *Yellow Stone* returned from her spring trip. Cabanné had come down from Council Bluff, to be in charge of the return voyage and possibly, as an old hand at such matters, to see the vessel through its inspection at Fort Leavenworth. The fact that the steamboat was bound only for Cabanné's post, just far enough to get past the army at Leavenworth, lends credence to this supposition.

Cabanné wrote Chouteau from St. Charles the first day out, saying the water was beautiful but getting lower. The crewmen were "adequate and sober," and Baptiste Dufond was at the wheel. Cabanné was about to pick up Daniel Lamont and John Dougherty, who had gone overland to St. Charles. The only other passenger known to be aboard was Jonathan L. Bean, subagent for the Yankton Sioux, with headquarters near the company's post called Fort Lookout.

Upon approaching the landing at Leavenworth on 2 August, the *Yellow Stone* nosed in and tied up, all hands apparently expecting the usual short stay and cursory inspection. Not until Lt. Jonathan Freeman, officer of the day, began to prowl about in the hold and count the whisky barrels carefully did Cabanné and Captain Bennett become aware that a new day had dawned in liquor control. What Freeman told them must have been startling. Word of the newest law had not reached the fort, but orders had come from army departmental headquarters, saying that the law of 1822 was now to be enforced, requiring the confiscation of all liquor being shipped specifically for Indian use.

Had William Clark or his clerk Maguire been paying more

attention to their mail, they would have found these same instructions. A circular had gone out from the Commissioner on 6 May, instructing all superintendents and agents to enforce the old act of 1822. If Clark had seen this notice, the *Yellow Stone* might never have left the American Fur Company warehouse with its cargo of a thousand gallons of whisky. The document must have been on the superintendent's desk long before he signed the liquor permit for this voyage.

Freeman found twenty-eight barrels (Cabanné said twenty-seven), but overlooked six. He transferred the liquor to the commissary stores to await further instructions from his commanding officer, Captain William M. Wickliffe. Meanwhile, it is likely that Cabanné, Bennett, Dougherty, Lamont, and Bean were in urgent conference with Wickliffe, who had been married two years earlier in Dougherty's home near the post. There was no room for compromise, although the army seems to have honored the additional ruling of 1828 that allowed enough liquor to sustain the crew during the round trip. That whisky was not, the officers said, to be left in the Indian country.

The furious Cabanné wrote Chouteau about the seizure, and in doing so revealed the basic stance of the St. Louis office toward the prohibition problem. In telling Chouteau about the six barrels that had been overlooked, he said, "In future we will oversee better." What he meant, of course, was We shall *conceal* better.

The steamboat headed north the next day, and when she had reached the Black Snake Hills and Robidoux's post, Cabanné was ready to write another agitated letter. He said he was sure that Narcisse LeClerc, an Opposition trader now traveling up the river in a keelboat, had been allowed to pass the Leavenworth inspection with more than his legal allotment of whisky.

LeClerc and a partner named Valois had been members of the Opposition in a small way. LeClerc had once worked at Fort Union, but had left for unknown reasons to begin operating in the country north of Council Bluff. His post was near Fort Look-out, a few miles above the mouth of White River. To complicate matters, that place was also the headquarters of Jonathan Bean, and the Chouteau people suspected that Bean directed some Sioux trade toward LeClerc now and then. It had not been a good year for LeClerc. During the winter, while traveling in the Ponca country to the Bad River, he had been robbed by a party of Sioux and his horses all killed.

Clark had given LeClerc a permit to transport 262 gallons of whisky, estimated to suffice as a year's supply for thirty-two employees. He was thus in Clark's eyes setting forth on the same basis as the Chouteau group. Soon after the *Yellow Stone* had cleared the Leavenworth inspection, LeClerc came along in his keelboat, the *Atlas,* his papers all in good order. He was carrying goods of his own and also some annuity goods (given annually to the Indians on the basis of treaty) for the Yanktons at Bean's agency. Lieutenant Freeman inspected the cargo, relieved LeClerc of four barrels, and let him proceed.

In the letter from the Black Snake Hills, Cabanné told Chouteau the story of the inspection and said he thought that Captain Bennett would be able to pick up the confiscated liquor on his return trip. "I am taking every possible means to avoid Leclerc's being able to ship [an excess]. He will be surveyed by land, as Robidoux is going to send about ten Indians . . . and if they meet with any [liquor] they will force those who are carting it to take it to the fort, and if they happen to avoid our surveillance there will be another inspection in passing Mr. Dougherty's." Cabanné's advantage was that Dougherty, traveling with him, had authority as a subagent to inspect LeClerc's goods. "All that our Company could desire," Cabanné continued, "is that the allowed quantity should not be exceeded and that it should be sent exactly to its destination."

Then Cabanné tipped his hand again, or indeed the company's hand. "But if we must have recourse to other means, I observe to you that the roads are passable only in autumn." Bring the liquor up the river by wagon, he meant, avoiding the inspectors.

At Bellevue, Dougherty went ashore to the new post he had been forced to occupy after living so long outside his jurisdiction. He had paid $1000 for the buildings at Bellevue formerly occupied by Lucien Fontenelle. Cabanné rode the *Yellow Stone* a few miles farther to his own post. The steamboat turned around there, starting back to St. Louis about 11 August.

When LeClerc reached Bellevue on 2 September, Dougherty inspected his liquor holdings and found eighty-four gallons of whisky, sixty of alcohol, and six of rum. As it was less than his permit called for, the agent was prepared to let him pass. But Cabanné had come down to witness the inspection, and saw aboard LeClerc's keelboat three deserters from his own post who had been hired by LeClerc. The altercation that was to follow started over these deserters, not the liquor question. At Dougherty's, Cabanné had drawn a pistol and taken the men prisoner, locking them in a storeroom from which they soon escaped. Two stubbornly returned to LeClerc's boat, which then continued upstream — carefully holding to the river bank opposite Cabanné's post as it passed that place on 5 September.

Unable to retrieve his deserters by shouting epithets across the water, Cabanné quickly formed a posse consisting of clerk Peter A. Sarpy and more than a dozen other employees. They hurried upstream by land, intercepted LeClerc, and took the two hapless deserters back to Cabanné. It was from these men, apparently, that Cabanné got the impression that LeClerc's goods had not been carefully searched anywhere along his route.

Now word came from St. Louis, no doubt from other boatmen, of the new law prohibiting *any* spirits in the Indian country. Cabanné decided to impose the new law on LeClerc personally, using his posse. The men overtook the LeClerc boat about 150 water miles upriver, confiscating not only the liquor but subagent Bean's annuity goods as well.

Dougherty reported the incident to Clark; LeClerc wrote strong letters of protest, demanding action against Cabanné; Clark wrote to Herring, the new commissioner. As Cabanné was a part of the American Fur Company, the many enemies and critics of that organization considered the affair one more evidence of its ruthlessness.

Clark now had the Cabanné-LeClerc altercation on his hands, besides the fact that the *Yellow Stone* had been caught at Fort Leavenworth carrying more liquor than the law allowed. Lieutenant Freeman brought the *Yellow Stone*'s liquor down to a St. Louis firm for storage, and called on Judge George Shannon in St. Charles for advice. In the curious way that tales of the West overlap, the Honorable George Shannon had been a youngster of eighteen on the Lewis and Clark Expedition, a quarter-century earlier, and now was a respected Missouri judge after studying at Transylvania University in Lexington, Kentucky. Judge Shannon felt the matter was serious, because the penalties for breaking the law of 1822 were severe — including the loss of a license to trade with the Indians. He recommended that Freeman take the matter to Clark and let the federal government handle it.

Clark reminded Secretary of War Cass of the 1828 order granting permits for the transporting of liquor for a trader's employees. He explained that he had given Chouteau a permit in good faith and had not learned of the new law until later. He felt that under the circumstances the kegs and barrels taken off the *Yellow Stone* should be returned to the American Fur Company.

As for Cabanné, word came from Washington in June 1833 that his license was to be revoked. Clark explained that the man had been trading under the company's license, already renewed. Did Herring and Cass want the *company* license revoked or only that of Cabanné?

The old trader should have known better than to get himself into such a predicament. Well educated in France, where he was born in 1773, he had been a trader for more than thirty years. He had traded in Spanish country and had smuggled furs into Canada in 1812 for Astor. The signs of his business acumen and his prosperity were his country homestead and his professional relationships in St. Louis, where he was a trustee of the town. He had been in charge of the Council Bluff post since 1819.

Despite his long association with the company, its officers did their best to pin the LeClerc matter on Cabanné alone. LeClerc had sued and won a judgment for $9200. Words of admonition had come from the New York office, William B. Astor saying the obvious, that Cabanné had no right to take matters into his own hands and had made the situation stickier by returning to his post for the winter before the matter was settled.

In the end, the company retained its license, to no one's surprise, and Cabanné was removed from the Indian country for a year. When the New York office refused to pay the judgment against him, it was paid by the Western Department. And no one believed that things would be much different in the age-old determination of the white man to ply the Indian with liquor.

When the *Yellow Stone* had stopped at Leavenworth for inspection, two Missouri physicians had come aboard for transportation up the river. They were part of the government's attempt in 1832 to extend the benefits of smallpox vaccination to all Indians under its jurisdiction.

Smallpox had scourged both the white and red populations again and again. But since 1796 the whites had been developing a weapon against the disease: a vaccination that transmitted the milder affliction called cowpox, which miraculously gave the human body immunity against the more serious smallpox.

In 1804, Lewis and Clark had, at Thomas Jefferson's insistence, carried cowpox "matter" into the unexplored western country to experiment with, but Lewis had decided his supply of the vaccine had lost its potency. In hit-or-miss fashion, the vaccination of Indians had continued anyway. In 1831, the Secretary of War had written to Indian agent John Crowell, enclosing vaccine matter he had obtained from the surgeon-general of the United States and suggesting that he should propagate more vaccine from the scabs of those Indians who contracted cowpox. In the same year, Dr. Thomas S. Bryant vaccinated 130 Indians under Clark's jurisdiction, asking fifty cents each as a fee. When the Indian bureau thought that was excessive, the doctor settled for twenty-five cents per vaccination.

Smallpox was quite prevalent among the western tribes in 1831 and 1832. The Shawnees in the Kansas area had it, and so did the Delawares north of the Kansas River; those tribes had been moved from the East by the government. The disease was ravaging the Poncas, as it did periodically, and was also affecting the Omahas farther up the Missouri. Cabanné had written to Chouteau in December 1831: "The smallpox is preventing all communication. . . . Never has this post shown such great destitution; the smallpox is ruining all our hopes." Dougherty visited the Pawnees in the fall and reported that he thought half the tribe would succumb. He said it had been thirty years since the disease had visited the Pawnees. The cycle of thirty-odd years seemed to be characteristic of smallpox; the survivors of the disease obtained immunity, and another generation was born to face the disaster anew.

In May 1832, Congress passed legislation meant to extend the benefits of vaccination to all Indians in a systematic way:

Be it enacted by the Senate and House of Representatives of the United States of America, in Congress assembled, That it shall be the duty of the several Indian agents and subagents, under the direction of the Secretary of War, to take such measures as he shall deem most efficient, to convene the Indian tribes in their respective towns, or in such other places and numbers, and at such seasons as shall be most convenient to the Indian population, for the purpose of arresting the progress of smallpox among the several tribes by vaccination. . . . *And be it further enacted,* That to carry this act into effect, the sum of twelve thousand dollars be appropriated out of any moneys in the treasury not otherwise appropriated.

Congress passed the bill with little debate, although Missouri congressman William H. Ashley thought that $12,000 was more than enough to cover the cost. There are indications in the records of the Commissioner of Indian Affairs that the law had been in prospect for some time; vaccine was ready for shipment a few days after the enactment, and the Secretary of War had a list of physicians who had applied for employment or were known to be willing. Cass had written in April to Dr. E. Jones, of Washington, D.C., that if the bill passed he would confine the selection of physicians to the districts where they were to do the vaccinating.

William Clark's connection with the project was slight and erratic, unlike his deep involvement in the whisky controversy. Agent Dougherty, to whom fell the task of coordinating the physicians' work in his jurisdiction, sent his reports and inquiries directly to Washington. Dougherty wrote Cass on 6 June that he thought $2000 would cover costs in his area. He estimated that with this sum he could vaccinate the Delawares, Shawnees, Kickapoos, Kansas, Iowas, Missouri Sauks, Otoes and Missouris, Omahas, Platte River Pawnees, Poncas, Yanktons, Tetons, and Ogalalla Sioux, Cheyennes, and perhaps the Arikaras. He doubted if he could take care of the Mandans without more money.

Hiring of physicians was handled by the War Department. The two doctors selected for the Missouri River region were both Missourians, Dr. David H. Davis (who at the same time applied for a later army or navy appointment), and Dr. Meriwether Martin. They were to receive $6 a day, including expenses, and were to report to Fort Leavenworth, where Dougherty would join them and help them plan their summer strategy.

Both doctors, waiting for the *Yellow Stone* when it arrived at Fort Leavenworth on 2 August, went aboard with Dougherty. They were thus silent witnesses to the search and seizure of the American Fur Company's liquor and to the rumblings that preceded the comic-opera vigilante operation of Cabanné. They left the steamboat with Dougherty at Bellevue, the plan being that Dr. Martin would remain in the area to vaccinate the Otoes, Omahas, and the large bands of Pawnees, while Dr. Davis would start upriver to treat the Indians farther north.

The summer went well for them. Despite predictions that the tribes would not accept the vaccine, and despite some agitation by trader Frederick Chouteau against the operation in the Kansas tribe that nearly cost him his trading license, everyone in-volved seemed satisfied with the project. Only the Santee Sioux refused to be vaccinated.

Dougherty sent a letter about the work to Cass in late autumn, enclosing the reports of the doctors. Dr. Martin had traveled from Bellevue — he does not say how — as far as Fort Pierre, vaccinating as he went. He had begun vaccinating the many Indians assembled at the fort in early October and had worked about two weeks in that location. He said he vaccinated about half the Indians he met, and his detailed roster contains the names and ages of 1056 persons. He added: "There has not been any smallpox among the Indians which I saw within the last thirty years, & I saw no other diseases among them." He would be willing, he said, to return and continue vaccinating during the following spring.

Dr. Davis wrote from Jackson, Missouri, but his detailed report to Cass has not survived with his letter. He had arrived at Leavenworth on 18 July to wait for the *Yellow Stone*. During the summer, he said, "I instructed the Indians how to vaccinate, the mode of preserving the matter, & furnished them with phials." His letter included this statement:

Owing to the advanced State of the Season, and the delay of the Indians of the various tribes vaccinated by me, it was found inexpedient by the agent to send me as high up as the Mandans. If it is your intent to send there in the spring and think proper to continue my appointment I would like you to advise me of it that I might embrace the opportunity of going up on the Steam Boat *Yellow Stone* in March or April.

Both physicians thus had indicated their willingness to finish their work the next spring. Between them they already had vaccinated about 3000 persons at a cost of $1800. Dougherty said in his covering letter that he was ready to proceed with the upper tribes if the government wanted him to do so. The Mandans and half the Arikaras remained to be treated, as well as the Hidatsas, living above the Mandans on the river.

The reply from Commissioner Herring must have surprised Dougherty, for Herring made it clear that he did not intend to finish the vaccination project. "If the Government should decide to complete the vaccination of all the Indians within your agency, which is not now contemplated, the necessary instructions will be transmitted to you." To Dr. Martin, Herring wrote at the same time: "It is not the present intention of the Government to prosecute this business. Should it be resumed you will probably be apprized of it in season to proffer an application for employment, should that be desirable to you."

Then Herring wrote to Cass, his superior, with a statement of how the fund for vaccination had been spent, enclosing an itemization in tabular form. "To some of the tribes the benefits of the act have not been extended. All however, which it is important should be done, may be accomplished the next season, with the balance of the original appropriation." He said it was not likely that the whole amount would be needed, and suggested that the residue of more than $4000 be applied to other needs of the department, "such as aid to emigrating tribes." This is a much more positive statement about completion of the work than he had given to Dougherty and Martin.

Section 4 of the vaccination law required that the War Department report to Congress on the results. Secretary Cass fulfilled this obligation by submitting an updated version of Herring's report to him, including the vague statement: "To some of the tribes, the benefits . . . have not been extended." He then suggested that the balance of the fund, now down to $3,807.50, be used to finish the vaccination *and* put at the disposal of the Commissioner for the relief of emigrating Indians.

To Congress, Cass was saying that some of the tribes had not yet been vaccinated but would be. To Dougherty and Dr. Martin the real intent of the Department was already known. "It is not the present intention of the Government to prosecute this business."

The conclusion of the vaccination episode is not a part of the *Yellow Stone* story and is chronologically beyond the scope of this work. It must be included, however, or the poignancy of the 1832 decision to discontinue vaccination of the Upper Missouri tribes is lost.

In the spring of 1837, the steamboat *St. Peters*, under Captain Bernard Pratte, Jr., made the annual spring trip for the Chouteau-Pratte interests, no longer a part of the American Fur Company. The vessel made the usual stops at Fort Leavenworth, Black Snake Hills, Council Bluff, Fort Pierre, Fort Clark, and on to Fort Union. Not quite a month after the stop at Fort Clark, clerk Francis A. Chardon recorded in his journal the death of a young Mandan from smallpox.

In later years, men would be searching their memories for the exact connection between the *St. Peters* and the outbreak. Parts of the story were by then already folklore. John James Audubon, repeating what he said Chardon had told him, wrote in his journal: "One Indian stole the blanket of another of the steamboat's watchmen (who lay at the point of death, if not already dead), wrapped himself in it, and carried it off, unaware of the disease that was to cost him his life, and that of many of his tribes — thousands, indeed." This is the tale that would stick in the minds of Americans, including historians, and be told and retold with variations. In 1977 historian Clyde C. Dollar would propose a different mode of transmission, based on a study of the known incubation period, time needed for symptoms to appear, and other factors. His conclusion is that the disease was carried by three Arikara women who boarded the *St. Peters* at Council Bluff after a visit with the Pawnees. The steamboat docked at Fort Clark on 19 June and the three women — recovering from smallpox but still carrying the virus in their bodies — disappeared among the Mandans.

No matter. That the disease was carried by the *St. Peters* is certain. A holocaust of ravaging disease broke out, not only among the Mandans but also among the neighboring Hidatsas. Because the steamboat had spent some time at the Sioux agency downriver, the havoc struck there also.

By 20 September, subagent William N. Fulkerson at the Mandan villages was writing to William Clark that "the Small pox has broken out in this country and is sweeping all before it. Unless it be checked in its mad career I would not be surprised if it wiped the Mandan and Rickaree [Arikara] Tribes clean from the face of the earth."

The Commissioner of Indian Affairs, who by now was C. A. Harris, had sent an inquiry about the rumors of smallpox, and Clark had forwarded it to Joshua Pilcher, subagent for the Sioux. Pilcher replied that he thought the disease was present in all the tribes from the Otoes on the Platte River to the Blackfeet in the Rockies, "and I have no doubt but it will continue until it compleats the transit to the Pacific Ocean."

Pilcher's solution was to vaccinate. "Competent persons must be employed and located at convenient points and remain until the prejudices, and superstitious notions of the Indians can be over come."

Correspondence in this vein was exchanged across the country, but the consensus was clear; vaccination would have helped earlier but that course now seemed too late. There seemed to be no sense of déjà vu in these letters, no tribal memory among persons who had participated in, or been witness to, the aborted vaccination program of 1832 that had ended at Fort Pierre and left half the Arikaras and all the Mandans untreated. Clark was still in office but had not been close to the 1832 program and probably knew nothing of its shortcomings. Pilcher had been on the Mississippi at the time. Secretary Cass and Commissioner Herring were out of office. John Dougherty, however, was still an Indian agent. In none of his surviving correspondence is there any sign that he spoke out to remind his colleagues of the failure of 1832.

In July, when the disease was at its worst in the Mandan villages, old Four Bears died. On the day of his death this man,

Mato-Tope or Four Bears, the influential second chief of the Mandans,
poses here for Catlin in his prized ceremonial garb.

highly regarded by many whites, allegedly delivered an anguished and bitter speech to his people. A transcript was found with Chardon's journal:

"I have never Wronged a White Man. . . . I have never called a White Man a Dog, but to day, I do Pronounce them to be a set of Black harted Dogs. . . . Think of your Wives, Children, Brothers, Sisters, Friends, and in fact all that you hold dear, are all Dead, or Dying, with their faces all rotten, caused by those dogs the whites, think of all that my friends, and rise all together and not leave one of them alive."

The epidemic of 1837 took lives in most of the tribes along the Missouri, in varying degree. It was far less severe in the tribes vaccinated by Dougherty's physicians, but obviously the doctors had not reached every individual. Among the tribes *not* vaccinated the destruction was catastrophic and the suffering immeasurable. The correlation between the vaccinating and the disease is too undependable to be figured exactly, but there is one certainty. The Mandans were not vaccinated and they are gone. By 6 February 1838, Clark could report to his superiors that "the Mandans consisting of 1600 souls had been reduced by the 1st of October last, to thirty one persons."

A bitter epitaph for an entire people was scrawled in the journal of Francis A. Chardon, who liked individual Mandans but despised as a whole the tribe that provided his livelihood. "What a bande of rascals has been used up."

Today there are no full-blooded Mandans on earth. *Exeunt omnes.*

———◇———

Long before the epidemic, steamboating on the upper river was showing signs of inevitable expansion. A proposal that Chouteau made to the New York office in the fall of 1833 may have been conceived at Fort Union, as he and McKenzie dined on buffalo tongues and held their Madeira glasses up to the candelight. Steamboating was the wave of the future and there was no turn-

When the boat's designation was added, this broadside notified potential shippers and passengers of a sailing. By changing the name, the printer could use the same engraving for other steamboats.

ing back, but the *Yellow Stone* would have to be replaced. Chouteau was going to ask the Astors how they felt about building a new steamboat.

By October, General Pratte would be in Cincinnati to sign a contract with shipbuilder Burton Hazen for the construction of another boat, to be called the *Assiniboin*. She was to be patterned after the *Yellow Stone,* length 120 feet, beam twenty feet, the hold six feet deep, but with a flatter and fuller hull than the older boat. The contract called for a "dead rise of four inches in sixteen foot in the sheer of the hull." For the comfort of travelers, a ladies' cabin with more amenities was to be built, and for the general welfare a barroom was added. The surviving contract is for the hull and other wood parts; there is no way of knowing whether an engine more powerful than that of the *Yellow Stone* was specified.

The New York office apparently did not approve the project before Pratte went to Cincinnati. William B. Astor's final approval was not penned until 17 October. It was reluctant and a bit stern:

Convinced as I am of the great advantage we derive from the aid of *steam* in supplying the wants of our remote posts on the Missouri, I fully concur in the propriety of our making the Steam Boat we use, as perfectly suitable for our business as may be practicable. And the experience of the two voyages has no doubt enabled you to pronounce judgment upon the fitness of the Yellow Stone for our purpose. I however should suppose that at the time of your return from the last voyage to the Upper Missouri, you were as well aware of the imperfections of our present boat, as on the 10th of September when you first mentioned your intention of building a new one; and I am disappointed in not receiving any intimation of the project, till so late a day, that the matter must be carried into immediate execution before I could express an opinion, or else be abandoned for want of time to ensure the completion of the vessel in due season. Believing that a new Boat of improved model will improve our interest, I have no objection to the construction of such a one, and will honour Mr. Pratte's drafts for the necessary funds. But after the arrival of the "Yellow Stone" from New Orleans next Spring, and the New Boat is ready to take her place, I recommend your selling the Yellow Stone, the first good opportunity that offers, as the company do not desire any further concern in Steam Boats, or other craft, than is absolutely necessary to the advantageous prosecution of our trade, and I presume we do not require two to do all, where Steam is required.

After signing the contract and conferring with the builders, Pratte feared that the new craft would not be ready in time for the annual spring trip in 1833. He advised Chouteau against selling the *Yellow Stone* for a while, and his advice was followed. So for a time the *Assiniboin* and the *Yellow Stone* were to be sister ships. Three years were to pass before the *Yellow Stone* would leave the fur trade.

As she was being prepared for another southern voyage, the vessel was involved in a small footnote to river history. Novelist and journalist Washington Irving had come west to try his hand at depicting the frontier. He and a traveling companion were approaching St. Louis in a packet from the Ohio River when their vessel collided with the *Yellow Stone*. Irving's friend, Albert-Alexandre de Pourtales, recorded the event in his journal: "Last night [13 September 1832] a large steamboat either intentionally or through unbelievable stupidity smashed its prow into our side. Another few inches and our wheels would have been broken, our ship would have been cut in two, and our shipmates drowned."

Only recently returned from several years in Europe, Irving probably did not know that the offending steamboat belonged to his friend of many years, John Jacob Astor. Neither could he have known at the time that within two years he would be hard at work on an account of Astor's ill-fated trading enterprise on the Pacific Coast. The collision may have provided an anecdote at the dinner table, when Irving later moved to Astor's rural retreat of Hellgate, in New York, to work on his famous classic of western history, *Astoria*.

4

Royalty on the Boiler Deck

◀€ THE GLUMNESS THAT HAD SETTLED over the company's staff because of the liquor ban was offset by the arrival, in the spring of 1833, of the new *Assiniboin*. Her slightly improved hull design, larger wheels, and better quarters meant that the *Yellow Stone* would be sold as soon as practicable. But for the single voyage now at hand, the two steamboats were to be traveling together much of the way, first one then the other in the lead, each crew available to assist if the other had trouble on the river.

Laidlaw had sent word from Fort Pierre that the mild weather had kept the buffalo out on the plains, so robes would be scarce. The scarcity of whisky only added to the poor prospect.

Chouteau, always probing for weak spots in the government's position, had asked the Indian Department for permission to take a limited quantity of liquor upriver this year. Commissioner Herring had written that the intent of the new law was clear and obvious and "the Prohibition is entire." Crooks had written Chouteau that "Gov. Cass is a Temperance Society Man in every sense of the word," fully behind the law. When Crooks had spoken with Cass early in 1832, before the law was passed, asking him to induce the British government to bar the use of spirits in the Hudson's Bay operation, he had sensed the hopelessness of the request.

A subtle difference between the business policies of Crooks and Chouteau was becoming apparent. Both believed in lobbying, wining and dining, and pressuring public officials in every way to obtain favors, concessions, and self-serving legislation. Yet Crooks seemed to have learned a basic lesson that Chouteau had not, for Chouteau would break the law when all else failed. Crooks lectured him on the futility of this course in a letter of 17 February 1833:

"It might be possible to elude the vigilance of all who watch your operation, and carry in a certain quantity of this liquid poison, but rely upon it that sooner, or later, detection will overtake you, and you will then deem all you have gained by it, too dearly purchased."

Crooks suspected that the British would decline the invitation to prohibit liquor in the Hudson's Bay Company operation, as a means of driving his own company out of business. "But still, if in the face of reason and common sense, the Executive will not have the law so modified as to afford us a fair chance with our Hudson's Bay opponents, I would (hard as it is) rather abandon the trade, than violate the statute if that was necessary to sustain ourselves against them."

Except for all the evidence that proves him otherwise, Pierre Chouteau, Jr., might appear obtuse and even stupid as he persisted in trying to get the liquor through. He wrote Clark to remind him that the contraband seized at Leavenworth was stored under bond, and asked if the company could take it upriver under that bond. In his more vigorous years, Clark might have loosed a string of harsh words upon Chouteau. Now he meekly forwarded the request to the Commissioner "as a courtesy to Chouteau." Predictably, Herring replied that the act of Congress left him with no discretionary power and the request could not be honored.

Word had come from New Orleans that the *Yellow Stone* was

leaving for St. Louis on 15 March, bringing all the trade goods that Chouteau had ordered from the East Coast and England except some casks of muscatel raisins, which were unavailable. Total cost of the merchandise was $5,812.95.

Insurance was then arranged, to cover the *Yellow Stone's* run as far as Council Bluff during a voyage of two months, amounting to $5000 for the boat and $20,000 for her cargo. And for the *Assiniboin,* $7000 to cover the vessel and $33,000 for the cargo. When Chouteau bought this coverage from the Missouri Insurance Company, he apparently thought the *Yellow Stone* would go only as far as Council Bluff as specified in the policy while the *Assiniboin* would proceed to Fort Union. In fact, the *Yellow Stone* was to ascend the river to Fort Pierre, presumably without coverage part of the way.

George Catlin's voyage on the *Yellow Stone* the previous year had set a precedent. For many years thereafter, the company would be taking selected passengers to the Upper Missouri. An example was the Nicollet-Frémont party of 1839, which would go to Fort Pierre, then travel overland on a surveying trip back to the Mississippi. Audubon traveled on the *Omega* in 1843. They were probably all paying passengers, although Catlin called himself the guest of Chouteau in his letters. The Nicollet-Frémont party paid the company $742.20 for four cabin passages and for six men sleeping on deck.

Sojourners on company boats were not always famous personages at the time of their voyages. Catlin's fame still awaited him. Nicollet would be remembered by scientists but unknown to a larger public. Frémont had yet to gain the notice that would make him a candidate for president and his name a household word many years later. Audubon, on the other hand, already had published *Birds of America* when he went up the river, and was well on the way to becoming one of America's best-known artists.

European royalty appeared now and then. Duke Paul of Württemberg made two trips up the Missouri before the age of the steamboat, one in 1822 and another seven years later, mak-

Maximilian and Bodmer, at right, meet the Hidatsas in this engraving of a Bodmer drawing.

ing scientific observations. Now the *Yellow Stone* was to carry another royal party, consisting of a prince who was also a scientist and soldier, accompanied by a hired artist, a "faithful retainer," and a dog named Spring.

Prince Maximilian of Wied-Neuweid was traveling under a pseudonym, calling himself Baron Braunsberg. Born in 1782, he was a short, pudgy man who dressed in green hunting clothes and looked forward to every new bend in the river with the zeal of an inveterate traveler. After studying at Göttingen he had entered the Prussian army and been captured by the French in 1806. By then he was an avid observer of natural history who was destined to return to Göttingen for further studies, rejoin the army to fight France again, and then begin a long period of travel in the Americas. First he had gone to Brazil, where his interests widened to include native peoples as well as plants and animals, and resulted in a two-volume publication when he returned to the ancestral palace near Koblenz.

His paid companion was a young Swiss artist, Karl Bodmer, immensely talented but more than a little out of place with his fancy attire, his parasol, and his musical snuffbox. The third member of the retinue was David Dreidoppel, Maximilian's body servant, taxidermist, and hunter. The three had sailed to the United States in 1832, arriving in Boston on Independence Day as "the salutes of artillery resounded from the coasts." Traveling slowly to savor the country, they had reached the Ohio River by September and soon took up temporary residence at the colony of scholars and writers at New Harmony, Indiana. Because of reports that cholera was appearing farther west, Maximilian spent the winter months at New Harmony, where naturalists Charles Lesueur and Thomas Say were his associates. Say had been west to the Rockies with the Stephen H. Long expedition of 1819–20. Not until Maximilian reached St. Louis in the spring did he decide exactly in which direction he wanted to go: west to the mountains or northwest along the Missouri to the tribes of the High Plains.

Captain William Drummond Stewart, a Scottish baronet from

Perthshire and a veteran of the Battle of Waterloo, was beginning a period of several years of wandering in the West. When Maximilian met him he was starting from St. Louis in a trading caravan going to the Rockies, and it seemed reasonable for the Prince to accompany him. But, as Maximilian wrote later, "after I had consulted many persons well acquainted with the country, the plan of following the course of the Missouri seemed to be the most suitable for my purposes; for, first, I should not be able to observe any Indians on the land journey . . . and, secondly, it is extremely difficult, nay impossible, to make considerable collections of natural history on such a journey."

The exploration he was planning had been influenced somewhat by the publication in 1814 of a narrative of the Lewis and Clark Expedition, written by Nicholas Biddle. In St. Louis, Maximilian now consulted with Clark himself. Clark's superb contribution to the Maximilian tour was a set of thirty-four maps, which his nephew Benjamin O'Fallon copied or traced from detailed maps drawn by Clark in 1804 between St. Louis and the Mandan villages. Nearly half of these maps were to survive in Maximilian's papers, at his home in Westphalia, to become the only extant maps covering 900 miles of the Lewis and Clark trek.

Although it is not always possible to tell what additional books and maps Maximilian carried because he added references to his diaries after he returned to Germany, he obviously had a small library with him. Some of the works he mentions in his diaries are François André Michaux, *The North American Silva* (Paris, 1819); Charles L. Bonaparte, *American Ornithology* (Philadelphia, 1825); Edwin James, *Account of an Expedition from Pittsburgh to the Rocky Mountains* (Philadelphia, 1823); John D. Godman, *American Natural History* (Philadelphia, 1826); and H. M. Brackenridge, *Views of Louisiana* (Pittsburgh, 1814).

Artist Bodmer had been known to Maximilian for scarcely a year. Admiring his landscapes of the Rhine and Moselle regions, the Prince hired him. Although he had little experience in por-

traying the human figure, Bodmer's Indian portraits are among
the finest ever made, while Maximilian's narrative, published in
German and translated into French and English, was to be
studied by scholars for a century and a half.

---◇---

Because no logbooks of the vessel have survived, and the only
other known diarist is Catlin with his general disregard of what
went on aboard, Maximilian's notes and narrative provide our
only detailed look at life on the *Yellow Stone*. The Prince was
interested in everything ashore and afloat. He did not always
understand what was going on, especially the machinations in
the fur trade, but he gives us data upon which to work.

Besides the royal party, the *Yellow Stone* carried the usual
group of Indian agents and company people. Chouteau and his
daughters and some friends rode as far as St. Charles, and when
they disembarked they were replaced by McKenzie and Dougherty. Sanford was aboard, no doubt bidding another lingering
good-bye to Emilie at the St. Charles landing. Dr. Benjamin F.
Fellowes, bearing a new commission as assistant military sur-
geon, was going to Fort Leavenworth on his first tour of duty.
Joshua Pilcher had joined the American Fur Company and was
going to take over at Council Bluff from the temporarily deposed
Cabanné.

Pilcher and Dougherty had been friends in the days when one
was a partner in the old Missouri Fur Company and the other
an interpreter for Indian agents. Pilcher's report that Dougherty
was a poor agent was on record with the Commissioner, and
Pilcher had nagged William Clark into ordering Dougherty
away from his comfortable home near Fort Leavenworth and
up to Bellevue where he really belonged. No doubt the two
avoided each other as much as possible on the crowded steamboat.

Maximilian estimated there were about a hundred persons on
board when the *Yellow Stone* left St. Louis at 10:30 A.M. on 10
April, the great flag flying at the stern and the company's pen-

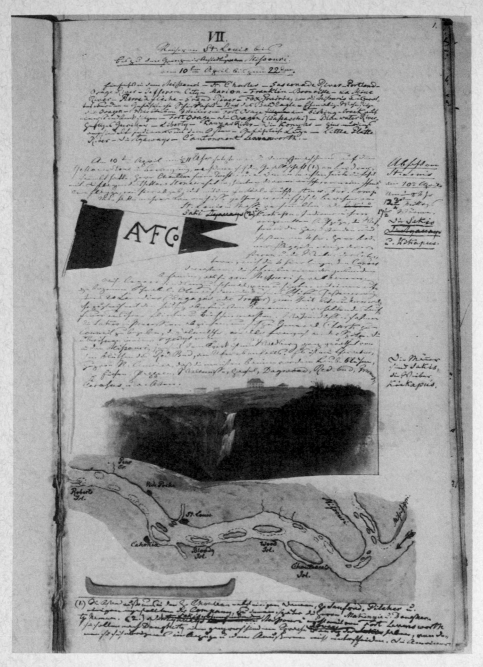

A section from one of Maximilian's diary pages, showing later additions in the margin. The red, white, and blue pennant flew from the jackstaff of the *Yellow Stone* on the 1833 voyage.

nant fluttering at the jackstaff. A party of Sauks and Kickapoos
waved from shore. The *engagés* aboard, some of whom were
drunk, kept up a roaring din of gunfire from rifles and shotguns.

In his first rush of enthusiasm for every observable detail of
his voyage, Maximilian wrote down the names of all the steamboats he saw as they left the St. Louis harbor, including the
*Halcyon, Illinois, Clinton, John Nelson, Utility, Paragon, Dove,
St. Jacques,* and the *William Parson.* He reported a stiff wind
from the west as the *Yellow Stone* turned to port and entered
the mouth of the Missouri, and he said the vessel ran all night,
providing more proof that steamboats customarily covered that
familiar part of the route in darkness. In the morning, the water
for washing and drinking was brown but, unfazed, he cheer-
fully judged it "cool and healthful."

The Prince started his collection of Indian memorabilia by
purchasing a Blackfoot scalp from an *engagé,* and he kept a
close eye on the shore for signs of spring as the *Yellow Stone*
left St. Charles. Redbuds were blooming before their leaves appeared; wild plums were white with blossoms. The forested hills
were just leafing out. The craft lay to at nightfall when it caught
up with the *Assiniboin,* which had left St. Louis first. *Engagés*
built a large fire on shore near Otter Island, "under the canopy
of the starry heavens," Maximilian wrote, while a pair of clari-
netists on board one of the vessels played Scottish airs and the
familiar "Yankee Doodle."

Next day they took on wood near the mouth of the Gasconade,
an area known for the quality of its yellow pine, and shot at
some wild turkeys. They passed the village of Portland, then
the mouth of the Osage River, and stopped at Côte sans Dessein,
an old French village almost destroyed by the river. Here Captain Bennett went ashore to visit his family and returned with
his wife and two half-blood Indian boys whom they were raising, to show them the boat.

On the following day, below Rockport, Maximilian saw two
towering rocks containing caves that reminded him of the ruins
of the castle at Heidelberg (they were passing the Manito

Rocks). He liked to compare what he was seeing and hearing with scenes in his homeland or in Brazil: The Independence River was "a brook like the Windbach"; and "On the hillside, the plum trees bloom instantly en masse here, just like our European fruit tree, the redbud just like our cherry tree." In the quiet upper country, where the sounds of wildlife were infrequent, he would miss "the varied voices of the parrots, the macaws, and many other birds, as well as of the monkeys and other creatures" of the South American jungle. Later he would observe, "The vast prairie scarcely offers a living creature, except now and then, herds of buffaloes and antelopes, or a few deer and wolves."

One day they stopped at Boonville on the left bank and bought cigars made from locally grown tobacco, and at New Philadelphia they bought a few reams of paper to use in drying plants. Captain Bennett showed Maximilian his own sketchy map of the river, which he kept to aid him and his pilot.

On 16 April, near Lexington, they reached a passage so shallow and dangerous that the engine was shut down and the boat pushed through by means of poles. At one point a cable was stretched to trees on shore, and the capstan was used to inch the boat forward. The next day, the engine failed and the captain lay to for repairs. The day after that, passengers wandered on shore until the bell summoned them back. This was not a day for making much distance. The crew sawed off snags, twenty men went ashore to pull the boat off a sandbar, but the line broke and the helpers fell down as in a game of tug-of-war. Later the rudder broke. On the morning of the nineteenth, a flatboat was obtained to remove some of the cargo so the *Yellow Stone* could float free, and Maximilian reported, "Mr. Bodmer made a faithful sketch of this scene." (See page 85.)

Dufond, the half-Ojibway pilot, met the boat near Liberty Landing, having come down in a pirogue, or dugout canoe, from Fort Union to assist during the remainder of the voyage. Maximilian described him as "a tall, slender, brown man . . . a half-

DAS DAMPFBOOT YELLOW-STONE. LE BATEAU A VAPEUR YELLOW-STONE.

THE STEAMER YELLOW-STONE

Better known than Bodmer's original watercolor (see jacket), this reproduction of the *Yellow Stone* aground on a sandbar has been altered somewhat by the engraver.

breed Indian, one of the best and most experienced pilots on the Missouri."

The vessel reached Fort Leavenworth on the morning of 22 April, after steering so close to the left bank that some hens enjoying the freedom of the decks escaped into the underbrush. Ignorant of the long history of liquor control, Maximilian wrote that the vessel was searched for "brandy," and that he had trouble getting permission to take enough to preserve his natural history specimens. "Several officers went back and forth all day," he said. "Our cabin was like a pigeon loft."

As the Prince saw the fort in 1833, it consisted of ten to twelve "nice houses" with verandas or galleries all around, and was garrisoned by four companies from the Sixth Infantry under Major Bennett Riley. John Treat Irving, stopping at the fort later in the same year, described it as having "About a dozen white-washed cottage-looking houses . . . so arranged as to form the three sides of a hollow square; the fourth is open, and looks out into a wide but broken prairie."

A new passenger came aboard here; subagent Jonathan L. Bean was bound for the Yankton agency.

Early the next morning, when the *Yellow Stone* had left the fort behind, a large branch lying in the river brushed the side of the cabin and pierced into the passenger compartments, carrying away part of a door jamb before it broke and dropped to the deck. "One might have been crushed in bed," Maximilian complained.

The Prince's natural history notes were keen and ample:

On the soil of the forest the *Podophyllum peltatum* [May apple] with its green leaves grew everywhere, and the color of redbud was marvelously beautiful. . . . Ducks everywhere on the river, mostly the wood duck which is very common here. By lunch time we land and hew wood in quantity . . . the forest soil was so densely overgrown with thick, tall rushes that one could not bring down a stick without breaking several. . . . Bodmer and Dreidoppel shot five parakeets.

Those birds, now long extinct, were Carolina parakeets that once inhabited the eastern United States in great flocks.

More problems occurred above the Grand Nemaha River. The vessel scraped bottom several times and ran aground in a storm. Out went the yawl for soundings, while a strong wind tipped the *Yellow Stone* on her side so dangerously that lines were stretched to trees lying in the water to prevent capsizing. One of the chimneys came down in the wind, and chickens (in coops, this time) were blown overboard and drowned. McKenzie later said it was the worst storm he ever had seen in the area.

At the Nishnabotna Narrows, where that river ran close to the Missouri, there was more unloading to do. The boat was aground again and would lose three days while waiting for a keelboat from up the river. Maximilian reported catfish weighing up to one hundred pounds, and flocks of white pelicans, often a hundred at a time, flying in wedge formations or semicircles. In the stomachs of the catfish the cooks found chicken bones, goose feet, and chunks of pork, all from the galley garbage.

Bodmer came back from his jaunts with specimens of red oak, ash, columbine, phlox, and once a live blue racer snake. He and Dreidoppel kept busy collecting for Maximilian. "Yesterday Bodmer brought back . . . a lovely orange-colored flower, *Batschia canescens* [hairy puccoon]" and Dreidoppel went hunting as often with his birding gun as with his rifle. The whole *Yellow Stone* party began to participate; Sanford and Dougherty came in with a raccoon and a white-footed mouse, and the skinned carcass of the raccoon was soon hanging at the stern with the rest of the fresh meat.

As the steamboat approached the mouth of the Platte, it passed Five Barrel Islands, which the French had called *Îles aux cinq barils* in honor of some long-forgotten incident in the eighteenth century. The islands would disappear within a generation or two, the name remaining but distorted in the stream called Keg Creek, which meets the river in Mills County, Iowa.

Lucien Fontenelle met the party here, having tired of waiting at Bellevue. A brigade leader, Fontenelle was taking parties of hunters and trappers westward into the Rockies annually and had been associated with the American Fur Company since

1830. After assuring himself that his goods were intact in the hold of the *Yellow Stone,* he would start overland for Fort Pierre, his point of departure for the mountains, arriving eight days ahead of the steamboat.

The Bellevue area now coming up had long been settled by isolated traders and was rapidly becoming the site of busy activities in both trading and Indian supervision. First came the new house of Fontenelle, who had sold his old one to the government and moved a few hundred yards downstream. Maximilian described the place as "a few buildings with lovely cornfields, situated before pleasantly green, densely forested hills." (He said that even a badly cultivated acre would yield a hundred bushels of corn, possibly an exaggeration for those days.) Above the Fontenelle house was the Bellevue agency, "quite prettily situated upon a summit, the cemetery entirely on the summit." There was nothing yet across the valley on the east bank, but within a few years there would be a settlement of Potawatomi Indians, uprooted from Indiana and Illinois, with their agent and a church mission. And a few years beyond that would come the twin cities of Omaha and Council Bluffs — the latter name was transferred from the west side by town-builders uncertain of where the old Council Bluff had really been.

Maximilian saw R. P. Beauchamp at Bellevue, serving as a subagent for Dougherty and of course bearing the usual honorary title of "major." Other permanent residents included a few *engagés* and blacksmith George Casner, who had tended the bellows and forge at Fort Madison and Fort Armstrong, on the Mississippi, as early as 1809 and now lived here with his family.

Maximilian reported a pleasant stop at Cabanné's post below Council Bluff. He casually mentioned that Pilcher had come to relieve Cabanné, but did not seem to know or care why. The traders and boat's officers spent some quiet hours sitting on a balcony with the Maximilian party, listening to frogs and whippoorwills and watching the Omaha Indians dance. About twenty Indians appeared before the house in the moonlight, danced an hour, and received a gift of tobacco. The leader of the group, a tall man wearing a headdress of owl tail feathers and pinions, was carrying a bow with arrows. His upper body was bare, painted in stripes, and he wore a breechcloth and leggins of painted and fringed leather.

A Rhinelander who loved nature could heartily enjoy a week in early May on the mid-Missouri, about where the states of Iowa, Kansas, Missouri, and Nebraska now come together. The mosquitoes would not yet have been up to regimental strength; the days would be sunny, the nights fragrantly cool. Sitting on Cabanné's balcony, Maximilian might have believed that the timbered hills rolled on forever and ever, although in fact there was bluestem prairie on either side of the bluffs not many miles away.

The Missouri can be thirty feet deep in this region, falling about a foot per mile and meandering through a valley that is often fifteen miles wide. The bluffs on either side of the valley afford protection for shade-loving trees, as do the many canyons cut by tributaries entering the river. The red oak and basswood stand in the best-protected slopes, while on the drier slopes and the high ridges grow the bur oak and bitternut hickory. The forest floor provides shelter for forty or more species of shrubs and such nonwoody plants as Solomon's seal, spring beauty, blue phlox, bloodroot, and blue and yellow violets. Willows prevail along the river's edge, and just behind them grows a heavy fringe of cottonwoods.

By early May, Maximilian could have found the maidenhair fern, trillium, and jack-in-the-pulpit. Butterflies would be showing up: the sulphurs, red admirals, and swallowtails. The pelicans that the Prince had recently seen would have been nearly the last, replaced as shore birds by the osprey, the great egret, and the green-backed heron.

A man boarded the *Yellow Stone* at Council Bluff who is not well known in history. Charles Howard Ashworth is not mentioned in the published editions of Maximilian's narrative, although he does appear in the field diaries. The two men chatted about the Missouri River Sauks, with whom Ashworth seemed familiar, and he claimed to be a midshipman in the British navy or marines. Perhaps the only place his name has surfaced in contemporary records has been in John Kirk Townsend's account of his travels with the Nathaniel J. Wyeth Expedition to the Oregon country in 1834. References to Ashworth are scant and uninformative, but apparently he joined Wyeth when he encountered the party at the Green River rendezvous of 1834. As yet, his other activities and his complete identity are undetermined. What was he doing at Council Bluff so early in the year unless he wintered there? Where was he going now, and what would he do until he surfaced in July 1834 at the rendezvous?

Bodmer's portfolio of sketches was bulging by now. He had worked hard since passing the mouth of the Platte, portraying the Otoes, Missouris, and Omahas. Maximilian packed his diaries with pages comparing these Indians with those of Brazil, often making sketches of his own to illustrate his comments. "They . . . made use in the dance of similar calabashes . . . like the Brazilian *Maracas* or *Tamaracas*, in which clattering stones are enclosed." When some Omaha women came on board, he described them as "clothed in red and blue with characteristic broad faces and large features, round fat heads, sagging breasts, small hands and feet. Their children had very dark brown hair but nice faces and snow-white teeth."

The long stretch of river between the Council Bluff and Fort Pierre was already known for its landmarks. Cabanné's post itself was not far below the remains of Fort Atkinson, the product of an unsuccessful scheme to send a government expedition to the Yellowstone in the 1820s. Now, in 1833, only ruins remained there, the chimneys and a stone building that probably had been the powder magazine. Sanford told Maximilian that he once found a mastodon tooth here and gave it to William Clark, an enthusiastic amateur paleontologist.

Now the hills were growing bare of timber and the underbrush was disappearing. No longer were the firemen tossing heavy lengths of hardwood into the firebox, but were resorting to cottonwood and willow. Wandering ashore, the travelers could gaze out from the hilltops and see endless prairie. There were no more snags in the river.

Letters came down from the *Assiniboin,* which was still ahead and which the *Yellow Stone* would not catch for another week. Woods Bluffs appeared on the west bank, near present-day Decatur, Nebraska, and then came Blackbird Hill, also on the west side, bearing the grave of the noted Omaha chief Blackbird. Maximilian wrote that this chief "was carried on mats, and his people dared not wake him loudly when he slept but rather tickled him with straw stems when he wanted to wake up." He had been buried "sitting upright upon a live mule, at the top of a green hill."

Many travelers passing what is now Sioux City, Iowa, made a respectful trip to the top of a knoll where Sergeant Charles Floyd had been buried in 1804. The young Virginian, who was the only man to die on the Lewis and Clark Expedition, had succumbed to what historians think was acute appendicitis. "A short stick marks the place where he is laid," Maximilian wrote, "and has often been renewed by travellers when the fires in the prairie have destroyed it."

Above the mouth of the James, where one of the rocky formations had been named White Bear Cliff by Lewis and Clark, the *Yellow Stone* came upon the *Assiniboin,* stuck in low water. A party from the older boat was invited aboard the new one by Captain Pratte, and Maximilian was struck by the differences between the two vessels. "In this steamer there were two cabins much lighter and more pleasant than those in the Yellow Stone; the stern cabin had ten berths, and the fore cabin twenty-four, and between decks was the large apartment distinct for the *engagés.*" The crew was keeping a pair of grizzly cubs aboard, having killed the mother.

Returning to his own quarters, Maximilian found that three Poncas had come aboard, the first he had seen. "They were all robust, good-looking men, tall . . . with strongly marked features, high cheek-bones, aquiline noses, and animated dark hazel eyes." No doubt Bodmer was sketching eagerly. There were days, here in the Dakota country, when the wind rocked the boat so much that Bodmer could sketch only with difficulty.

Still unable to move, the *Assiniboin* stayed behind to be assisted by a keelboat while the *Yellow Stone* went on. But there were other delays, including a stop to cut red cedar, when the two boats spent the night near each other. Cedar Island delighted Maximilian, who called it "a beautiful, dark, dense wilderness of slender cedar trees sixty or more feet high, the rough bark of which was hanging down in strips." Here McKenzie ordered thirty or forty young cedars felled and peeled to make tentpoles for use at Fort Union.

The wildlife was changing; the first pronghorn was seen above Cedar Island, and next day a sighting of the first buffalo stimulated a hunting party to go ashore. Another stretch of bad water was to delay them for five days, and once the weather was cool enough to require fires in the cabin stoves.

As he traveled, Maximilian was following Catlin's letters to the *Advertiser*. And, like Audubon a decade later, he would find them inaccurate and misleading. He and Bodmer already had inspected many of Catlin's paintings in St. Louis and had formed strong opinions about them. Perhaps the Prince was already formulating in his mind the review that he would publish in the journal *Isis* in 1842, deriding some of Catlin's observations. He would entitle it "Einige Bemerkungen über Geo. Catlins Werk: Lettres and notes on the manners, customs and condition of the North-American Indians."

Maximilian credited Catlin with collecting useful material, but said that much of it needed "rectification," and he resented Catlin's use of the customary term *red* for the complexion of the Indians, saying they were brown. He disputed Catlin's statement that poisoned arrows were used, and disagreed with Catlin's feeling that the Mandans were somehow "nicer," even whiter, than other Indians. They were allies of the Americans and thus were viewed differently, he claimed. And of course he thought that Bodmer's portraits were accurate and authentic while Catlin's were not, and that Catlin's vocabulary lists were faulty.

Continuing upstream, the *Yellow Stone* caught the *Assiniboin* at the foot of the Bijoux Hills at present-day Chamberlain, South Dakota. Here the *Yellow Stone* got stranded again and had to lie to. Bodmer went ashore with Jonathan Bean to see the Sioux agency at Fort Lookout. For the rest of the travelers it was a wretched interlude, with both steamboats and even the *Assiniboin*'s keelboat aground. Captain Bennett had the crew stride vigorously from port to starboard, back and forth, in an effort to rock the *Yellow Stone* loose. Everyone aboard was unhappy because the boat was stranded in midstream, while the *Assiniboin* was near the right bank of the river and the crew could go ashore to bowl on the sandy shores or practice target shooting.

Bodmer, however, was ecstatically viewing the Sioux he found at Fort Lookout, especially a statuesque man of about sixty called the Big Soldier (see page 94). The full-length watercolor he made of the Big Soldier was to become one of the best-known Indian portraits of all time. Here is Maximilian's description of the man:

His face was painted red with vermilion, and with short, black, parallel transverse stripes on the cheeks. On his head he wore long feathers of birds of prey, which were tokens of his warlike exploits, particularly of the enemies he had slain. They were fastened in a horizontal position with strips of red cloth. In his ears he wore long strings of blue glass beads, and, on his breast, suspended from his neck, the great silver medal of the United States. His leather leggins, painted with dark crosses and stripes, were very neatly ornamented with a broad embroidered stripe of yellow, red, and sky-blue figures, consisting of dyed porcupine quills, and his shoes were adorned in the same manner. His buffalo robe was tanned white, and he had his tomahawk or battle-axe in his hand.

Now the boats had to navigate the Great Bend or Grand Detour, the place that disgusted every boatman because a person

Wahktageli, a Yankton Sioux warrior called Big Soldier by the Americans, poses here for what was to become Bodmer's most famous Indian portrait.

on foot could walk across the neck of the bend in an hour and a half, but keelboats and steamboats had to go the long way by water. Usually the captain would put twenty or so men ashore at the lower entrance to the detour with instructions to walk across and start cutting wood. From nine to ten hours later, depending on the stage of the river, they would be picked up again.

On 30 May, Fort Pierre came in sight and the flags were broken out as the usual gunfire began. Everything seemed new, from the peeled logs of the stockade to the recently riven shingles on the roofs. In only a year old Fort Tecumseh, just downstream, had become an isolated, decaying old house, no doubt robbed of its good timber for the construction of the new post.

Fontenelle had arrived as expected, and now his brigade departed for the mountains, a party of sixty men and 185 horses. It seems reasonable to speculate that young Ashworth was a member of the group. It is a loss to the world of art, natural history, and ethnography that Maximilian and Bodmer did not accompany Fontenelle. They might have done so, had they known how the summer's activities among the trading parties would evolve. Fontenelle reached the Horse Creek fork of the Green River, west of the Wind River Mountains in southwestern Wyoming, in mid-July. Already in progress when he arrived, the last great trappers' rendezvous had brought together men from all the mountain fur companies. Participants included Captain Benjamin Bonneville, Robert Campbell, Thomas Fitzpatrick, Andrew Drips, many small operators, and large numbers of Indians from the mountain tribes.

At the end of the rendezvous, two separate parties headed north to avoid hostile Arikaras in the valley of the North Platte. Maximilian and his companions could have attached themselves to the trains of Bonneville or Campbell, both of whom took their furs to the Yellowstone for transport to St. Louis. By accompanying one of these parties, Maximilian's group could have resumed its original itinerary, visiting Fort McKenzie briefly and returning downstream to the Mandans. In the course of the summer the trio would have covered much territory not yet traversed by naturalists or artists. A Bodmer painting of the Wind River Mountains might have been spectacular.

While the *Yellow Stone* prepared to return to St. Louis, Maximilian and Bodmer wrote letters to their European friends, made journal entries, and sketched the Teton Sioux who had come in from the plains. Their baggage was transferred to the *Assiniboin,* with its ladies' cabin and other comforts, for the trip to Fort Union 600 miles upstream. From there they would go by keelboat to Fort McKenzie at the mouth of the Marias, staying nearly five weeks studying the wilder tribes — Blackfeet, Piegans, Assiniboins, and Crees. At the end of September they would descend to Fort Clark to winter among the Mandans and Hidatsas as guests of McKenzie and local manager James Kipp. By now they had become such amenable companions to the traders that when Maximilian asked about winter quarters at Fort Clark, McKenzie ordered a separate cabin to be built so the painting and study could go on uninterrupted.

Maximilian's party was not to return to St. Louis until the following spring, traveling in a mackinaw boat with a crew of boatmen and two grizzly cubs they had acquired during the winter. From there they would make a leisurely trip through the East before setting sail for home.

By 21 June the *Yellow Stone* was back in St. Louis. Although she had departed the landing at Fort Pierre for the last time, her career was far from finished. The association of the Astor and Chouteau interests was, however, about to end. The old man was in Europe when he wrote to Chouteau just three days after the steamboat had arrived home:

"Wishing to retire from the Concern in which I am engaged with your House, you will please to take this as notice thereof, & that the agreement entered into [i.e., renewed] on the 7th. May 1830 — between your House & me on the part of the American Fur Company will expire with the outfit of the present year on the terms expressed in said agreement."

5

Last Trip on the Missouri

❧❡ MARK TWAIN WAS NOT THE FIRST kid who hung around the landings of river towns, watching the smoke leave the blackened steamboat chimneys and, on rare occasions when he was invited to come aboard, learning the art and lore of piloting.

PILOT: "And what's the worst thing can happen, savin' a real disaster?"

BOY: "Gittin' aground, wouldn't it be?"

PILOT: "Nope. Try again."

BOY: "Runnin' outa wood, then?"

PILOT: "Gittin' close, but it's worse'n that. Once more."

BOY: "I gotta give up."

PILOT: "Goin' aground in midriver *and* runnin' plumb outa wood. That's the absolute worst. I remember one time . . ."

And he would be off on a long yarn about the awful things that could happen to a hapless pilot and his crew.

Joseph La Barge was such a waterfront lad, but with a powerful advantage over other youngsters who haunted the wharfside in St. Louis. Both of his brothers, John B. and Charles S., were

97

steamboat pilots. Almost all we know of young Joseph's early years on the river is to be found in a narrative written about him seventy years later by historian Hiram M. Chittenden, *The History of Early Steamboat Navigation on the Missouri River*. Mainly a biography of La Barge, this work can be relied upon for an account of his later years when he was pilot and captain for the American Fur Company and other shipping firms. Some of his memories of his earlier years, however, do not jibe with the facts. It is as if he had got some of his life mixed in his memory with that of his older brothers.

According to the Chittenden narrative, La Barge's first schoolmaster was Jean Baptiste Trudeau, and he studied at Trudeau's home on Pine Street, later attending St. Mary's in Perry County. He reported signing on as an apprentice clerk when the *Yellow Stone* went south for the winter in the fall of 1831.

During the first winter that the vessel ran in the bayous above and below New Orleans and on the lower reaches of the Mississippi, La Barge's heritage made him especially useful as an interpreter in the sugar trade around Bayou la Fourche.

In the spring of 1832, on the voyage that carried Catlin and set a distance record on the Missouri, he was allegedly aboard and bound for Council Bluff, where at the age of seventeen he went to work for Cabanné as an *engagé*. His recollection is not supported by any document in the Chouteau papers, including the lists of passengers and company employees. He also recalled that he returned to St. Louis on business in time to board the *Yellow Stone* for her second voyage of 1832. He said he was a member of the armed party sent by Cabanné to confiscate the liquor on LeClerc's keelboat, but his name is not among those on a memorandum of 11 January 1833 from LeClerc to William Clark, naming the twenty-two members of the posse. He further claimed to have been employed on the *Warrior* under Captain Throckmorton when it carried troops up the Mississippi and attacked the fleeing Sauks. He could not have done this and participated in the vigilante episode on the Missouri, for the two events occurred too close together. The first appearance of

This medal, issued by Chouteau, was intended to be a close imitation of the medal issued by the government that bore the President's image, as a token of friendship and alliance.

This small artillery piece, with a bore of one and a half inches, served on American Fur Company steamboats, possibly the *Yellow Stone*.

Joseph's name in the payroll records of the company is in Ledger R, showing that he earned $66 for the period 9 July to 3 October 1833. The amount was charged to the Upper Missouri Outfit, not the *Yellow Stone*.

Two things are certain about the young La Barge: he was definitely aboard the *Yellow Stone* when she departed St. Louis on her voyage up the river in the summer of 1833, and he had by then acquired a respectable amount of knowledge of how a steamboat was operated. Now he was about to learn about the scourge of cholera.

———◆———

Russel Farnham, who had been an Astorian on the Columbia and walked across Siberia with dispatches for Astor, and who now had a partnership with George Davenport to represent the American Fur Company on the Upper Mississippi, visited St. Louis in October 1832. Two hours after the onset of symptoms, he was dead of cholera.

In its way, it was a disease more dreaded than smallpox. You could be vaccinated against smallpox, you could even survive a mild attack and gain immunity, but cholera was implacable. And it was not always so mercifully quick as in the case of trader Farnham. First came diarrhea and painful cramps, violent vomiting and resulting dehydration. The victims' faces became blue and pinched, their arms and legs cold, the skin of their hands and feet puckered from loss of body fluids. It was not thought of as a disease (there was no germ theory at the time) but as a kind of malaise in the air. If you were of a religious turn, you might even consider it a scourge. The editor of the *Western Sunday School Messenger* called it a rod in the hand of God, raised to strike down "drunkards and filthy, wicked people of all descriptions."

Recommended cures were many. Eat no vegetables except potatoes, and avoid the night air. Try whisky or camphor vapors. Burning tar or pitch was a favorite; in New Orleans there were clouds of smoke everywhere as the torches flared.

Doctors were helpless, too. Some recommended bloodletting, that old standby for nearly every ill, but the most universally used remedy was the mercuric compound calomel, a laxative. Massive doses brought on more diarrhea and consequent dehydration. Dr. Lewis F. Linn of St. Louis advised drawing up to half a gallon of blood, followed by a compound of calomel, camphor, and cayenne pepper until "relief" was obtained.

Cholera was a Far Eastern pandemic, appearing in the United States for the first time in the nineteenth century in the years 1832, 1833, and 1834. Once gone, it did not return to North America until the winter of 1848–49. It traveled by rail, canal, and steamboat. Like typhoid fever, cholera is spread from organisms in the human digestive tract by means of contamination such as sewage in the drinking water or the handling of food with unclean hands. The killing aspect of the disease is dehydration. When scientists came to this conclusion in the twentieth century and began to administer glucose to help the body retain water, the outlook for cholera victims worldwide began to improve. For the victims of 1833, living in conditions that were basically unsanitary, the scourge simply had to run its course.

The involvement of the *Yellow Stone* in the cholera-ridden areas along the Missouri River can be documented by newspaper accounts and contemporary correspondence. As usual, our only information about La Barge's role in the story comes from his own lips, the recollections of an old man long after the event. Still, it has the ring of truth.

Early in July 1833 the *Yellow Stone,* steaming on the Missouri below present-day Kansas City, was struck by cholera. Everyone in the crew reportedly died except Captain Andrew Bennett and La Barge. Leaving young Joe in charge of the vessel, Bennett set out for St. Louis to recruit another crew. ("My crew has died of cholera," one can almost hear him saying. "How would you like to ship on as clerk? You'll have to travel four hundred miles to get to the boat.")

As La Barge recalls it, "There is a spot just below Kansas City . . . where I buried eight cholera victims in one grave."

He then began his long watch as the only person left on board, while news of the *Yellow Stone*'s plight spread throughout Jackson County. A journal kept by Isaac McCoy contains this entry for 13 July: "A boat had, a few days ago, been compelled by Cholera to stop on her way up. Some eight or ten had died. She stopped, and is still lying about 5 miles from our house. Our neighborhood is considerably uneasy."

A delegation of frightened Kansas Territory men approached the steamboat and advised La Barge, from a safe distance on shore, that they would burn the craft to the waterline if it were not moved at once. La Barge told his biographer that he fired up the boilers and maneuvered the *Yellow Stone* away from shore, piloting her upstream and across to the west bank of the Missouri, above the mouth of the Kansas.

When La Barge related this tale to Chittenden he was an old and seasoned pilot. Chittenden himself had spent long years on the western rivers as an officer in the Army Corps of Engineers. Apparently neither man thought the story of a semitrained pilot firing up a steamboat and navigating it across the Missouri to a safe mooring was beyond reason. If it happened, it must have involved much scampering up and down the stairs from the pilot-house to the engineer's station — and incredible luck during the docking procedure.

As there was cargo aboard for the Chouteau post on the Kansas, La Barge set out on foot for instructions about its disposal. A guard stationed near the post because of the cholera scare turned him away, but took a message to his employer. As La Barge was preparing to spend the night on the prairie, a former school friend, Edward Ligueste Chouteau, visiting at the trading house, brought him food and a buffalo robe to sleep under. Next day he was back at the *Yellow Stone*, no doubt keeping alert on the one hand for deputations of alarmed Kansans and on the other for the return of Captain Bennett.

According to La Barge's recollections, the *Assiniboin* came down the river from its trip to Fort Union but would not stop at his signal because Captain Pratte feared the cholera. After a long delay, Bennett returned from St. Louis with a new crew, aboard the steamboat *Otto* in the hire of rival traders Sublette & Campbell. The *Yellow Stone* then went on, and there is no known diary or other account of the journey. By now these voyages had become routine. When the boat arrived at Bellevue in August, cholera had already reached the little settlement. Dougherty at Bellevue and Pilcher upstream at Council Bluff both survived, although Dougherty had been gravely ill. About eight persons died, including subagent C. G. Clark, blacksmith George Casner and his wife, and interpreter Francis Sansoucier.

On a visit to Leavenworth in August, the Rev. W. D. Smith heard that cholera had been carried to Bellevue by the *Yellow Stone*. Pilcher, however, told Chouteau that the disease had appeared in July. Pilcher had been dashing back and forth between his post and the Bellevue agency, nursing the sick. Apparently he and Dougherty had learned to be good neighbors, for the two lived in the same house during the height of the disease. Cool weather brought an end to the outbreak.

During the next appearance of cholera on the Missouri in the summer of 1851, La Barge would have an occasion to recall his adventure on the *Yellow Stone*. By then he was captain of the *St. Ange*, chartered to the American Fur Company and en route to Fort Union, when cholera appeared on board. This time he would reach his destination routinely, but with a death toll of fourteen passengers and crew.

———◇———

Kenneth McKenzie was easily frustrated and was in a frustrating business, but he had the wits to arrive at ingenious solutions when plans did not turn out well. The man who had conceived the idea of using a steamboat while still working with dog teams was quick to respond to the new liquor law of 1832. Some traders had begun to haul their whisky along the Santa Fe Trail by wagon for some distance, then cut back to the Missouri above Fort Leavenworth to elude inspection. McKenzie was not in a position to engage in such a feint, so he decided to put technology to work for him once more. He would build a distillery at Fort Union and make whisky on the spot. He would thus not be "transporting" it into Indian country and perhaps not be perceived as violating the law. As the idea of a man whose frustrations were beginning to show, it had flaws but it was worth a try.

A visit to New York and Montreal during the winter of 1832–33, with a stop in Pittsburgh to take delivery of the *Assiniboin,* had given McKenzie a splendid opportunity to buy the copper tubing, vats, and other paraphernalia for making an "alembic" for distilling alcohol. His demeanor in New York had given his superiors in the company the impression that he was depressed by the effects of the new liquor law. Crooks wrote anxiously to Chouteau soon after McKenzie left the East Coast: "I was really sorry to see him depart with prospects of the future so discouraging in relation to his trade; but it was wholly impossible to affect the least modification as regards the use of ardent spirits in the Indian country."

Crooks had other preoccupations now, having decided that he would try to purchase all the American Fur Company except the Western Department. This was not a time he would have chosen for another debacle in the company with all the unpleasant public outcry that might ensue.

It was clear that Secretary Cass intended to enforce the new law. In May 1833 he sent a circular to all his superintendents and agents, restating the statutes then in force regarding liquor and the Indians. His message, harking back to both the original act of 1802 and the one of 1822, went into the mail while the *Yellow Stone* and *Assiniboin* were laboring upstream; one of the boats was even then carrying the parts for the distillery. Later McKenzie was to declare that he had taken the equipment on the *Yellow Stone* for a man from the Red River of the North, planning to keep it at Fort Union until the owner could pick it up in a cart.

His plan assumed that some corn would be available from the Indians, especially the Arikaras and Mandans, who were a farming people, and that more could be got from Council Bluff.

In case this was not enough, McKenzie had put several men ashore on the left bank of the Missouri, across from Aowa Creek, which joins the river in present-day Dixon County, Nebraska. They were to start what Maximilian had seen vaguely as a "plantation." This party of farmers led by François Roi could not have expected a crop the first year; by the time they could break the soil and prepare it for planting the season would be too far along to make corn in 1833.

Indian corn was a better bet. When the *Yellow Stone* stopped at the Yankton village, Maximilian duly reported in his diary that McKenzie scolded the Indians there for not raising more corn — perhaps wondering why it was any of McKenzie's business how much corn they raised. Only Chouteau and a few other company men would have understood McKenzie's motive.

At Fort Pierre, McKenzie transferred his mysterious collection of coils and vats to the *Assiniboin* for the final leg of his trip to Fort Union. Once there, he assembled a distillery and began his moonshine project. The St. Louis office knew about the operation and McKenzie spoke slyly of it in his letters to Pratte and Chouteau. The code word was "wine." "Could I hope for the pleasure of a visit from you I could regale you with a glass of genuine Fort Union wine," he wrote General Pratte. He said that 200 lodges of Crees had gone north because they "did not like the wine." To Chouteau he wrote, "Our manufactory flourishes, we only want corn enough to be able to supply all our wants." To Pilcher at Council Bluff: "I hope you will be able to furnish me with a good supply of corn in the Spring or my wine vats will be empty."

Possibly McKenzie thought he saw two loopholes in the law. He was making whisky, not transporting it; and he was calling it "wine" on the assumption that the law banned only "ardent spirits," meaning something stronger than wine.

The Crees may have disliked what McKenzie was dispensing by the late fall, but the Assiniboins apparently loved it. Robert Campbell, building a rival post about four miles from Fort Union, wrote in his journal that "McKenzie gives as much whisky as the Indians can drink for nothing. Barrel after Barrel he sends all around amongst the Indians and these will not trade otherwise." He also said that McKenzie was telling the Indians he would kill their dogs if they took their trade elsewhere.

What better way to entertain a fellow trader, on that rare occasion when one dropped by, than to break out the best of the homemade whisky? In late August 1833, before the product of the alembic had even aged in the wood, two guests arrived at Fort Union and were welcomed by McKenzie. One was Michel S. Cerré, a St. Louis trader scarcely thirty years old, who was in training for a life in frontier commerce. He had been to Santa Fe and had been a partner in an enterprise meant to rival the American Fur Company. Later the Astors had done the usual and bought out the operation. Now Cerré was returning from an expedition with Captain Benjamin Bonneville.

The other visitor was Nathaniel J. Wyeth, of Massachusetts, who had made a career selling ice in Boston but was now determined to establish a fur trade on the Pacific Coast. He was returning from his first overland trip to the Columbia. Wyeth's journal entry upon leaving Fort Union mentions the distillery but gives the impression that he thought it was a legitimate circumvention of the liquor laws. He describes McKenzie as a most polite host, and adds: "Here they are beginning to distil spirits from corn traded from the Inds. below. This owing to some restrictions on the introduction of the article into the country."

When Wyeth arrived home he wrote to a newspaper about his experiences. "Among the American Traders I have received much attention from Mr. McKenzie and Mr. Laidlaw of the Am. Fur Co. and Mr. Wm. L. Sublette. To all the above gentlemen I tender my thanks."

These are not the words of a man bent on mischief. But how does one describe a descent of the Missouri, and royal treatment at Fort Union, without mentioning that distillery? Considering its location, it was a wondrous piece of equipment, demanding some notice. Wyeth left Fort Union on 27 August and was at

Fort Leavenworth by 27 September. There, perhaps while dining at the officers' mess or chatting with the post commander, Wyeth apparently mentioned the distillery. Or was it Michel Cerré, onetime rival of McKenzie's company, who first let the word out? No matter. What happened ruined the distilling game and infuriated McKenzie.

McKenzie reasoned that one of the two guests had informed on him. Gone now was the cool logic with which McKenzie reasoned, or pretended to, that he was not breaking the law. He was simply gambling that government officials would not find out about his distillery.

He wrote these lines to Chouteau after the storm broke:

It is true that Mr. L. Ceré & a person who introduced himself to me as Capt. Wyethe were at Fort Union in August last, they were both very ernest in their applications to purchase liquor of me, I had none to sell them but offered them wine which they declined buying altho they drank freely of it at my table during their stay; notwithstanding which I am informed the said Capt. Wythe was beastly drunk during his voyage down the Mo. & mortified at my refusing him liquor, & being moreover a man of such dissipated habits, it seems to me that any statement of his should be listened to with extreme caution. Neither does it surprize me that L. Ceré who was judged unworthy of being engaged by A.F.C. (his brother also being dismissed from their employ) should under feelings of mortified self love make any statements that he thought calculated to injure the A.F.C.

McKenzie's disclaimer, written to a man fully aware of the circumstances, seemed to be prompting Chouteau to deny the existence of the distillery and discredit Wyeth and Cerré. And Chouteau did try to bluff the matter through. Writing to William Clark, 23 November 1833, he said that any distillery operated as openly and unlawfully as Clark had described in a letter of inquiry was unknown to the company. The report was probably greatly blown up, perhaps even wholly unfounded. Still, Chouteau remarked, there was just one little thing that Clark ought to know: "The company, believing that a wild Pear and Berries might be converted into wine (which they understand not to be prohibited), did authorise experiments to be made." Anything other than this experiment — which Chouteau seems to have conceived as his own personal embellishment to the story — would have been stopped immediately by the St. Louis office, he said.

Chouteau was in the East, involved in the prospective purchase of the western division of the company, when news of the McKenzie *contretemps* became public. Off he went to Washington with protestations, obviously disturbed that such a mess had developed so soon after the Cabanné highjinks had almost cost the company its license.

Crooks was far from sympathetic and was especially derisive of the notion that McKenzie thought he could keep his operation secret. He wrote Chouteau that, "if you do use the article [the still] it will be known generally, much as if you published it in the *Missouri Republican*." Some action or position of Clark's had disappointed Crooks, and in the same letter he said,

Clark too was a very dear friend of yours, and you would almost have knocked a man down who dared to question his sincerity. But that is better understood now, & the parties duly appreciated I trust at least. Do not place yourself in the power of the Government agents in the hope that they will construe things liberally, for you may depend upon it, they will seize with delight every opportunity to annoy you.

McKenzie's embarrassment dampened but did not extinguish his zeal for fur trading. It also prompted Congress to deal specifically with his kind of scheme. A new trade and intercourse act of 30 June 1834 forbade anyone in the Indian country to "set up or continue any distillery for manufacturing ardent spirits" on pain of a thousand dollars fine and the destruction of the still by military force if necessary.

No one seemed to recall, or had the inclination to find out, that McKenzie was in violation of a law already on the books. He and the company were lucky that Judge Shannon in St. Charles, or Commissioner Elbert Herring in Washington, or perhaps some bitter enemy of Astor and his people, did not focus attention on the act of 3 March 1815, written as if the lawmakers had McKenzie himself in mind:

Sec. 20. And be it further enacted, That any person who shall, after the thirtieth day of June next, erect, or cause to be erected, any still, or boiler, or other vessel used or intended to be used in the distillation of spirituous liquors, or who shall so use any still, or boiler, or other vessel, in any part of the United States beyond the then existing boundary line established by law between the United States and the Indian tribes, or who shall be the owner, agent, or superintendent thereof, shall forfeit and pay the sum of five thousand dollars, together with the said still, boiler, or other vessel, and the spirits distilled therein; one moiety of which shall be for the use of the informer, and the other for the use of the United States.

Certainly Wyeth and Cerré could not have known of this substantial informer's fee when they drank from McKenzie's casks at Fort Union.

Ordered down the river by Chouteau, McKenzie went to Europe and visited Prince Maximilian. Returning to St. Louis in 1835, he renewed his business connections with Pratte and Chouteau, later buying out Chouteau's interest in a commission firm. He was to become a wholesale grocer and later an importer of wines and liquors. He was still involved in the fur business, however, and when an early winter disrupted transportation on the Upper Missouri he was at Fort Union in apparent control. And he was still his old, acerbic self. "It is a mortifying reflection," he wrote the office on 10 December 1835, "after spending so much money in Steam boats the whole Summer should be too short to transport goods from St. Louis to this place, and that this Company should be subject to the derision of our pittiful opponents."

———◇———

When the *Yellow Stone* left St. Louis in early July 1833 on its final Missouri River run, Justin Williams of Boonville was on board and learned that the steamboat might be for sale in the autumn. "I have come to the conclution to buy her if she can be had on terms that will corispond with me (or rather our) circumstances," he wrote Chouteau. He asked whether the company really wanted to sell, and the price and terms of payment. His partner was to be "a Mr. Thomas, well known to Captain Bennett."

In the autumn, Captain Bennett moved his gear to new quarters on the *Assiniboin* and became its master. His berth on the *Yellow Stone* was taken by E. P. Austin. The company was sending both boats south for the winter, the *Yellow Stone* to New Orleans and the *Assiniboin* to the Yazoo country. It was time to re-enroll the *Yellow Stone,* and Captain Austin had been instructed to get her papers in order at New Orleans. This time she was to be enrolled not as the property of the American Fur Company, but of Jean Pierre Cabanné. It was a curious piece of business, for obviously Cabanné did not purchase the vessel. It may have been a gesture to the old trader, who had been barred from the Upper Missouri for a year and needed some kind of responsibility. Or it may have been a ploy to keep the steamboat off the firm's inventory, now that B. Pratte & Co. was about to separate from the American Fur Company.

So Cabanné, whose other preoccupation at the time was building a house in town to supplant the one he had occupied since 1820 at the eastern edge of Forest Park, became the "owner" of a contraption he had once held in disdain. There was a problem in enrolling it in New Orleans, however, for he was not a resident of Louisiana (*enrollment* was the term used for licensing, if a vessel was larger than twenty tons and engaged in coastal or inland water trade). Captain Austin sent the papers up to Chouteau, saying they should be processed in St. Louis where there was now a port of entry and a customs house.

In the spring of 1834, the American Fur Company underwent a wrenching change. John Jacob Astor, now ill and — some historians say — forever disillusioned about the future of the fur trade, already had notified his St. Louis partners that he wanted to terminate that relationship. He sold his ninety percent of the company and retired. Crooks bought the Northern Department, retaining the firm's name and its headquarters in New York and Michilmackinac. The Western Department was sold to its St. Louis operators and became Pratte, Chouteau & Company. The change gave Chouteau the position and recognition he had earned as general manager of the western operation, and no doubt Crooks was glad that the unpredictable and ungovernable Chouteau was no longer his to fret about.

By early April 1834 the *Yellow Stone* was back in St. Louis, with a different destination and cargo. She would no longer work on the distant frontier, but in the mainstream of Mississippi River commerce. Instead of being the only steamboat within a thousand miles, she was one of 127 that went up the Mississippi in that year as part of the lead-mining trade centered around Dubuque, in present-day Iowa, and Galena in Illinois.

Before the white man came, Indians of this area were mining the lead by carrying the ore in baskets to a hole scooped in the earth, where it was mixed with burning wood. The molten lead was drained into a second, shallower hole to harden into chunks or "pigs." Early whites built side-hill log furnaces and hired Indian women to carry ore to them. At about the time of the War of 1812, it was thought that if the Indians could be persuaded to stop producing furs and turn all their attention to lead mining, the British traders in the area would withdraw and stop proselytizing the Sioux, Winnebago, Sauk, and Fox tribes. It was not to happen. Now that the Black Hawk War and its subsequent treaty had opened the region to settlement, the mines were passing from Indian to Caucasian hands. The miners no longer were Indian women, but tough men from Derbyshire and Cornwall, and from Ireland and Germany, who had learned the trade in their homelands. Smelting techniques were becoming less crude, and the lead market was prospering when the fur trade was not.

On her second trip up the Mississippi, the *Yellow Stone* was chartered to carry the defeated war chief Black Hawk and his party from Rock Island to Prairie du Chien, in Wisconsin Territory, on government business. By now the old chief was infirm and no longer a power in his tribe, and in the little time left to him (he would die in 1838) was rapidly becoming Americanized. He lived in a log house and liked to reminisce about his trip to Washington and the East Coast, including some time spent as a prisoner at Fortress Monroe in Virginia to "punish" him for the war that bore his name.

In August the *Yellow Stone* was crammed with cargo again for a trip to New Orleans — making her last trip out of St. Louis as a Chouteau steamboat, with the burden she was built for: neatly tagged packs of buffalo robes, deerskins, and beaver pelts.

A group of buyers found her at last in the spring of 1835. On her enrollment papers filed at Vicksburg, Mississippi, on 15 May, were the names of owners John P. Phillips and the firm of Martin and Askin, of Vicksburg; and William Adams, of Natchez. Phillips was her new captain.

Because of the *Yellow Stone* the Missouri River frontier would never be the same. The traders would go on cursing the problems of steamboating, as William Laidlaw was still doing in 1839: "I really do think that unless we can get a steamboat more adapted for the river . . . we had better give it up." Traders would go on wishing for a vessel of truly shallow draft while purchasing a succession of medium-draft boats like the *Trapper*, which in 1841 drew more than five feet fully loaded. They would endure one disaster after another, such as the burning of the *Assiniboin* in 1835, just below the mouth of the Heart River in what is now North Dakota, with the loss of not only her usual cargo but also much of Prince Maximilian's natural history collection, which had not yet been sent to him. In the same year, the *Diana* sank after being snagged, at a place still called Diana Bend near Lexington, Missouri. In 1839 the *Pirate* sank below Bellevue. But steamboating and the fur trade — indeed *any* trade on western waters — were now intertwined.

To readers of the *New Orleans Bee* who kept an eye on the shipping news, the *Yellow Stone* was now just another frequent caller at the port, bringing sugar products from the bayous below the city or coming down from the upper country with cotton and produce. Her captains changed from Austin to Watt to Grant, and her stopovers bore the names of tiny landings like Tehula and Leflores. She arrived once in August from Louisville carrying flour, butter, corn, potatoes, apples, tobacco, and 151 dozen chickens.

The French ambience had been strong in St. Louis, but New Orleans was a more thoroughly French city. To the citizens of that city the steamboat was a *bateau-à-vapeur,* moving along the waterfront among vessels called *bricks* (brigs), *bateaux de remorque* (towboats), or *goéls* (schooners). Her cargo might include anything from *farine pour boulangers* (flour) to *graines de jardinage* (garden seeds), all stowed in *barriques* (casks), *paniers* (hampers), or *caisses* (boxes).

The *Yellow Stone* had freighted this kind of miscellany up and down the lower reaches of the Mississippi for less than six months when her Vicksburg-Natchez owners decided to sell her. Perhaps they got an interesting offer or perhaps they sensed that the vessel was old, as steamboats go. The average life of such a boat was five years, and the *Yellow Stone* had lived hard. Her bow had fended off many an ugly, gray snag, and her bottom had scraped across vast acres of underwater sand. The prairie winds had scoured her fittings like sandpaper; her main deck was pitted with tiny black holes made by coals blowing from the open firebox. She had survived in one piece, however, and had not become a sunken landmark with a river bend named after her crushed hull. She was alive and worth saving.

In the fall of 1835 the *Yellow Stone* was sold to Thomas Toby & Brother, of New Orleans. Heavily engaged in intracoastal trading, the Tobys had connections in the Mexican province of Texas, shipping goods to and from landings all along the Gulf. Thomas Toby was president of the Louisiana Insurance Company and the Orleans Navigation Company.

No 105   Permanent

IN PURSUANCE of an Act of the

Congress of the United States of America, entitled " An
Act concerning the registering and recording of Ships or
Vessels. " *Thomas Toby of New Orleans
State of Louisiana*

*having taken or subscribed the Oath required by the said Act
and having affirmed that he is the true and*

only owner of the Ship or Vessel called the **Yellow Stone**
*of New Orleans whereof J. W. Crimson
is at present Master and a* **CITIZEN** *of the United States,*

as he hath sworn

*and that the said Ship or Vessel was Built at Louisville in the
State of Kentucky in the year 1831 as it also
appears from the records of this Office shewing
an Enrollment No. 48 issued on the 15th day of
May 1835, not now surrendered but proof made
the same is lost or mislaid. Property changed.*

*And said Record
of Office having certified that the said Ship or
Vessel has one Deck and no Mast and that her
length is One hundred twenty two feet one Inch,
her breadth Seventy feet six Inches,
her depth Six feet one Inch,
and that she measures One hundred forty four and
8/95th. tons,
that she is a Steam Boat has a square Stern two chimnies
and two cabins and an Alligator head;
And the said Thomas Toby having
agreed to the description and admeasurement above specified, and sufficient security
having been given, according to the said Act, the said Steam Boat
has been duly registered at the Port of New Orleans*

GIVEN *under our Hand and Seal at the Port of
New Orleans this twenty ninth day of December
in the Year One Thousand Eight Hundred and thirty five*

A certificate of 1835 that authorized the *Yellow Stone* to trade in the
foreign waters of Texas. Note that the ship pictured in the upper
left corner of the certificate, labeled *Yellow Stone*, is a
sailing ship, not a steamboat.

In November the *Yellow Stone* was "hauled up" at a New Orleans shipyard for major repairs and rebuilding. We know that the work was done by Harrod & Hughes, and that Charles Harrod was another of those multi-interest entrepreneurs who shipped, stored, performed commissions, and was secretary of the Marine and Fire Insurance Company. All we have, however, to tell us what work was done on the *Yellow Stone* is a single invoice, so badly worn that not all of it can be deciphered. It is to be found among the Grayson Papers at the Library of the Daughters of the Texas Republic, at the Alamo. In the following transcription of the document the symbol [ ] indicates material that cannot be read:

[   ] *Boat Yellow Stone & Owns. to Harrod & Hughes   Drs.*

Hauling up & Launching		$550.00
5153-½ feet cypress Lumber	4½	231.91
2463 " 2 inch cypress Plank	4	98.52
979 " cypress scantling	3½	34.26
1446 " ½ Inch Y. Pine	3	43.38
1174 " Y. P. Scantling	3	35.22
[ ] Oak timber for rudder stock 18 [ ]	$1	18.00
[ ] " for timbers 8 12 x 5 40 ft	6¼	[ ]
[ ] " for rudders 5.8.5 ea. 34	6¼	[ ]
[ ] " for stem [ ]	6¼	2.19
4 Oak Knees @ 4.16 4 do. @ $3 12		28.00
1 ps Oak timber 5 8 x 11= 37 ft	6¼	2.31
1 do do for Stantions 24 4 x 15= 130 ft	6¼	8.12½
19 Oak Plank 1265 feet	6¼	79.06
20 Y. P. do 1072	5	53.60
5 Y.P. sticks timber 177 feet	62½	110.62½
6 Oak Logs 20 ft in 120 "	50	60.00
47 feet Boat Plank	31	14.57
25 Y. P. Slats for guards	25	6.25
2 poplar Gunnels for pillow blocks	$4	8.00
8 [ ] trennels	[ ]	.50
450 lbs. Oakum @ 45 mops $2		47.00
2 Bbls. Pitch	4	8.00

231 ½ wrot Spikes 18 lb wrot nails	16	39.92
623 lb Cut Spikes 351 lb cut nails	8	77.92
2 ps. Oak timber 28 12 x 12 [ ] 56 ft	50	28.00
[do]		16.00
[	]	19.11
2 Bots Japan $2 ¾ lb. Letharge 19¢		2.19
318 days carpenters	3.25	1033.50
152 ½ caulkers	3.25	495.62
18 ¼ Labourers	2.00	36.50
125 " Joiners	3.25	406.25
40 " Superintendance	3.00	120.00
1 Boat	35.00	3719.15
35 feet Oak for do 2.19 nails 40 lbs. 2.59		37.59
1 mast		5.00
For Boat & Materials [ ] bill Labour		39.76
[		]
4 Mo. Interest on 2360		59.00
		3860.50

New Orleans Dec. 30th 183[5]
Recd. payment viz:

By Cash $1500
Draft on Thos Toby & Brother 2360 — 4 Mo.
Harrod & Hughes

It cannot be determined from this invoice alone what altera-
tions or repairs were made on the *Yellow Stone*. The work was
not a minor repair job, for it required dry-docking and forty days
of "superintendance." The cost of nearly $4000 is almost equal
to the original estimate of the contractor who built the vessel
in 1830–31.

In steamboating it was not uncommon to build a new boat
around an old but serviceable engine. Something of this nature
may have been done to the *Yellow Stone*. Although the bill of
materials does not suggest a complete new hull and superstruc-
ture, it does suggest drastic replacement of vital wooden parts.
There is much wood in 2463 feet of two-inch cypress planking,

whether the clerk who drew up the bill meant running feet or board feet.

Perhaps the decks that had felt the soft tread of Sioux and Mandan moccasins, the thud of Creole jackboots, and the gentle pad-pad-pad of Maximilian's dog Spring were not the same decks that bore the crew of the refurbished *Yellow Stone*, now relaunched in southern waters for the rest of her life.

6

---·—◆—·---

Down on
the Brazos

◄◖ IT TOOK LESS than forty-eight hours for a traveler to go
from New Orleans to Galveston by steamboat, and somewhat
longer by schooner. However, this is a deceptive statistic, for
not everyone wanted to reach only Galveston or Velasco or
Quintana on the Gulf of Mexico. But in the earliest days of
Texas settlement, a family determined to move there with their
wagons, animals, household goods, and farm equipment looked
for the kind of navigable waters they had known in the valleys
of the Ohio and the Mississippi.

Equally important as getting to Texas was finding a way to
ship the products of Texas back to markets in the United States.
A farmer who once had hauled his wheat and corn to a Louisville landing and put it aboard a flatboat or steamboat, bound
for the port of New Orleans, might find upon moving to Texas
that what looked like a wondrous network of rivers on the map
was really just a series of shallow and sluggish streams. They
were dry part of the year and available mostly to the people on
the lower reaches near the Gulf.

The problem was to be solved partly by steamboats: first the
Ariel, which began to run on the lower Rio Grande in 1829 be-

fore coming to the Brazos, then the *Cayuga* and the *Laura,* and in 1836 the *Yellow Stone.*

Of the Americans bound for Texas, historian Ray Billington has said that "the same inner urge which drove Missourians to Oregon in the 1840s impelled them to migrate to Texas in the 1820s. In short, Texas lay athwart the westward path from Tennessee as did Iowa and Nebraska from Ohio. The American colonization of Texas was a normal and natural feature of the age-old American tradition of pushing on toward the Pacific."

In the decade of the 1820s Texas had been an empty land that the Mexican government was eager to populate with Americans. They came individually, or they followed twenty-seven-year-old Stephen F. Austin, who had taken up the dream of his father, Moses Austin, of founding a settlement in Texas. His grant, achieved with much delay and vexation, permitted him to introduce 300 families into Texas and assign them land. As their *impresario* he received a small commission from every transaction, in return for which he not only obtained the land but founded the town of San Felipe de Austin and served as a very young father figure to the emigrants. The original settlers — the Old Three Hundred honored in Texas history — attracted others. About 2000 settlers had come by 1825, bringing more than 400 slaves.

As other colonization went forward and the population grew, it soon became evident that Americans who were willing enough to become citizens of Mexico were not finely tuned to the Mexican culture. The supreme role of the church and certain concepts of government bothered them. They were bothered, too, by the good old American notion that *they* were superior. That they would one day take Texas from the Mexicans seemed as inevitable as the fact that other Americans were inexorably taking the Trans-Mississippi from the Indians. This idea would soon have a name: Manifest Destiny.

The Brazos River and the settlements at its mouth were becoming a lively and vital area. About the lower third of the Brazos was navigable in varying degrees. The very lowest reaches, those leading into the Gulf, were tidewater and mercifully free of shoals. Quintana and Velasco, at its mouth, were tidewater towns. Farther upriver were Brazoria and Marion, beyond which the water became difficult and only seasonably navigable. The absolute head of practical navigation was at Hidalgo Falls, above Washington-on-the-Brazos. Along both banks, and reaching many miles inland where the soil was right and roads could be built to the river, were cotton plantations. Getting this cotton to New Orleans and shipping supplies to the plantation owners up on the Brazos became the business of several entrepreneurs at the mouth of the river. McKinney and Williams, a growing firm at Quintana, had brought the Louisville-built *Laura* to the Brazos. Until then, getting steam power to the river had become an urgent campaign, with many citizens of the area signing subscription papers that promised financial gain to anyone who would operate a steamboat in the area.

Thomas F. McKinney, a former Missourian like Austin, had engaged in the Santa Fe trade out of St. Louis and was one of Austin's enrollees. His partner, Samuel May Williams, was a man with much commercial experience and many contacts, including some in Latin America, and had been Austin's secretary and business partner for a decade.

When these men formed a partnership in 1834, the political climate in Texas was stormy. Mexican leaders had begun to fear they had opened the gates too wide. Even before Andrew Jackson's election to the presidency, the United States had offered Mexico a million dollars for Texas. With the 1828 election of Jackson, a man with expansionist views, the apprehension grew. A colonization law of 1824 had been generous to those Americans who promised to become loyal citizens and Catholics. A new law in 1830 was more provocative, forbidding further settlement to "citizens of foreign countries lying adjacent to the Mexican territory."

For a time the seizure of power by the Mexican Federalist party in 1832 calmed the growing unrest of the colonists. They thought the party and its leader, General Antonio López de

Santa Anna, would implement their cause. But Santa Anna continued to move to the right in political terms, soon becoming an avowed leader of the Centralists he had defeated. By 1834 he had proclaimed himself president of Mexico forever, sent the congress home, and replaced the highly regarded constitution of 1824 that had given the Americans a degree of freedom and self-government.

Santa Anna had invaded Texas and begun to disarm and subjugate its American residents when the *Yellow Stone* came to the Brazos. She had been registered in New Orleans in December 1835, the term *registration* meaning that she was scheduled to operate in foreign waters. For the next year and a half she would give every appearance of belonging to the firm of McKinney and Williams, but she was registered by Toby & Brother and there is every indication that the Tobys continued to own her. Later, her United States registry would prove to be an advantage. On 31 December 1835, she cleared the port of New Orleans with Thomas Wigg Grayson as captain and headed for Texas. On her decks were forty-seven young men comprising the Mobile Grays, coming— like other volunteers from all over the United States — to oppose Santa Anna.

Picture Sam Houston sitting on a camp chair in front of his tent, squinting into the morning light that ricocheted off the waters of the Brazos. The river was in flood. Tied along the bank, perhaps with a hawser looped over a half-buried snag, was the *Yellow Stone*. The steamboat had been moored at Jared Groce's landing just upstream, taking on cotton, when Houston had bivouacked his army at the river's edge on 31 March 1836. Now, a couple of days later, he had pressed the vessel into the service of the Texas Revolution.

Back in 1831, the year the *Yellow Stone* had made her first run up the Missouri, Houston was living among the Cherokees, drinking too much, quarreling, and losing face with the tribe that had given him love and trust in the days when he had been

ARMY ORDERS.

———————*———————

Convention Hall, Washington, March 2, 1836.

War is raging on the frontiers. Bejar is besieged by two thousand of the enemy, under the command of general Siezma. Reinforcements are on their march, to unite with the besieging army. By the last report, our force in Bejar was only one hundred and fifty men strong. The citizens of Texas must rally to the aid of our army, or it will perish. Let the citizens of the East march to the combat. The enemy must be driven from our soil, or desolation will accompany their march upon us. *Independence is declared*, it must be maintained. Immediate action, united with valor, alone can achieve the great work. The services of all are forthwith required in the field.

SAM. HOUSTON,

Commander-in-Chief of the Army.

P. S. It is rumored that the enemy are on their march to Gonzales, and that they have entered the colonies. The fate of Bejar is unknown. The country must and shall be defended. The patriots of Texas are *appealed to, in behalf of their bleeding country.* **S. H.**

Houston was at Washington-on-the-Brazos and the Alamo was under siege when this call for volunteers went out.

their agent and advocate. The presence of the steamboat could not have failed to remind him of another America — the highlands and the Rockies — and of his lost dream of establishing a colony at the mouth of the Columbia. Texas was a new career for him, trying to take this wild country from Mexico, and it was new for this vessel now transformed from a thundering voyager of the North to a slogging old cotton packet of the tidewaters. The next three weeks would put them both into the history books.

Like so many westering adventurers, Houston was a Virginian, born in Rockbridge County in 1793. After his father's early death Sam's mother had taken the family to Tennessee, where Houston learned to know the Cherokees. He served in the army, became a friend of Andrew Jackson, and crammed a legal education into six months of study. Then came two terms in Congress followed by two terms as governor of Tennessee.

When his personal life went awry — his wife left him in 1829 — Houston drew closer to the Indians. Serving them as agent and advocate, he traveled often between Washington and the frontier. After some of his trips had taken him to Texas, he decided to remain there, becoming a strong voice among the settlers who were trying to find a way of solving their differences with the Mexican government. When the showdown erupted, he was named commander-in-chief of the army of Texas, an appointment that had now brought him to the swampy banks of the Brazos.

Houston's advance that looked like a retreat (and so it seemed to many of his volunteers) began a hundred or so miles to the west at Gonzáles on 11 March. The bad news awaiting him there, along with about 275 new troops, was that the Alamo probably had fallen. Publicly announcing his disbelief, he proceeded privately as if that disaster at San Antonio actually had happened; that Santa Anna and about 5000 soldiers had finally overrun the little garrison of less than 200 defenders. He got word to Colonel James Fannin at Goliad, another doomed bastion southwest of San Antonio, to vacate that place and join him in the relief of the Alamo. Then he decided he lacked the strength to meet Santa Anna. After burning the town of Gonzáles, he set off eastward toward the Colorado River, where a more populous area would enable him to build up his fighting force.

After lingering here to increase his army from 1200 to 1400 men, and considering for a time the wisdom of taking out after Mexican general Joaquin Ramírez Sesma, who was not far away, Houston unaccountably began to fall back eastward again toward the Brazos. Meanwhile, ugly news came from Goliad. Colonel Fannin, failing to withdraw in time, had surrendered to a thousand Mexicans. The commander who had made the capture, General José Urrea, had recommended clemency for the prisoners. Instead, Santa Anna had ordered them shot to death on 27 March.

So much disheartening news, so little progress against Santa Anna, had sent panic through the hearts of the settlers. A general flight toward the safety of the East, later to be called the Runaway Scrape, was under way. When he reached San Felipe on the Brazos, Houston found his effective force of soldiers reduced by half. Surprising his officers and acting against their advice, he led his men up the river instead of heading downstream, where he was more likely to meet the enemy. At Groce's cotton plantation, about twenty miles up the Brazos, he had gone into camp on 31 March.

At this time there was no plan to proceed farther east in what would have given further appearance of a retreat. The enemy, Houston and his men thought, were downstream. When word came to Houston that the *Yellow Stone* was at Groce's Landing, being loaded with cotton, her usefulness became obvious. What better way to descend upon the foe, with the river at flood-tide, than to be led by a smoke-belching, roaring steamboat carrying artillery, horses, and riders, and followed on both banks by riflemen shouting "Remember the Alamo!"

On the first of April, Inspector General George W. Hockley reported to T. J. Rusk, the Texas Secretary of War:

The weather for the last four days has been wet, and the men have undergone great fatigue from that circumstance and the road being in many places almost impassable for our waggons — so soon as they can wash their clothing and arrange their arms an entire organization of camp duty & discipline will be established. . . . The Steam Boat Yellow Stone captn. Ross is at Groce's landing taking in cotton. The Commander in Chief directed her to be taken in charge for the use of the army in case it should be necessary to descend the river rapidly to act upon the enemy. Maj. [William G.] Cooke and a sufficient guard are now on board and she will be detained until her services can safely be dispensed with. She is nearly loaded with cotton.

———◆———

The spirited young men calling themselves the Mobile Grays, who had come to Texas on the *Yellow Stone* only a few weeks before, had been the most dashing collection of passengers the old boat had ever carried. They had hung over her guard rails, watching the Gulf waters race past; had raised their glasses in honor of free men and a free Texas when they gathered in the forward cabin for meals; and had polished their rifles in the sun on the rolling hurricane deck. Now they all were dead, executed at Goliad, and there was little to show that the *Yellow Stone* had been for a short time a troop ship astir with the vigor and laughter of eager soldiers.

Even her assignments had seemed dull since that promising beginning. She had carried a few volunteers upriver from Quintana, and operators McKinney and Williams had billed the Texas government seventy dollars. When the *Laura* was snagged below San Felipe, the *Yellow Stone* was sent to pick up the cargo and deliver it to Washington-on-the-Brazos. When she arrived at her destination she was no longer commanded by Thomas Wigg Grayson but by Captain John E. Ross, who was also her pilot.

Ross had come down from Tennessee and was involved in maritime matters at least by 1832, when he was master of the

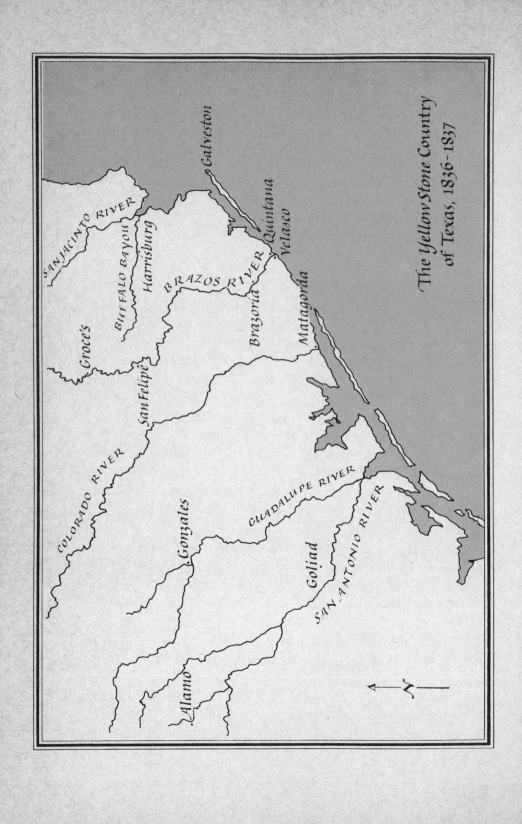

The Yellowstone Country of Texas, 1836–1837

SAN JACINTO RIVER

BUFFALO BAYOU

Harrisburg

BRAZOS RIVER

Groce's

San Felipe

COLORADO RIVER

Galveston

Quintana

Velasco

Brazoria

Matagorda

GUADALUPE RIVER

SAN ANTONIO RIVER

Gonzales

Goliad

Alamo

N

Exert. He had brought the little steamer *Cayuga* to Galveston from New Orleans in 1834.

The engineer was Lewis C. Ferguson, who appears later as captain of the *Correo* in 1838. The clerk was James H. West of South Carolina, who would in less than a year become captain of the *Laura* and gingerly maneuver her up the hazardous Buffalo Bayou to the new settlement called Houston.

Robert Hall, a deckhand, had come to Texas with the *Yellow Stone* and was later to serve as a Texas Ranger and a soldier in the Confederate Army. Another crewman, Thomas Lubbock, was the brother of future governor Francis W. Lubbock. He was to become a famed Indian fighter and the colonel of a Civil War regiment.

Other crew members included deckhands John McKinney, Dyer Horton, and James Ferns; firemen William Cooke, M. M. McLain, Martin Shackles, Ira Tate, and Thomas Smith; stewards Robert Mosely and Mrs. Mosely; second steward Ira Armstrong; and cook Benjamin Sherman.

It is not surprising to find that some of these people were solidly committed to the Texas struggle and willing to play a role in it. Others had mixed feelings. Not only was the *Yellow Stone* a vessel of United States registry, but none of her crew was a Texas citizen under Mexican law. Suppose the vessel were to be captured. Would the captain and crew be considered prisoners of war or merely common buccaneers?

Another mental reservation appeared, one considered not quite honorable at a time when the fate of the Alamo was still so fresh in the minds of incensed Texans. Some of these crewmen appear to have asked, "What's in it for me?" However distasteful the question at the time, it had to be addressed before the *Yellow Stone* could be of use to General Houston. The result was this letter of 2 April to Captain Ross from Houston:

Sir: You and each member of your crew and the Officers of the Boat are hereby assured and guaranteed that they and Each of them shall be indemnified as well as the boat Owners for Wages, losses and damages in consideration of the impressment of your Boat into the public Services of Texas (the Yellow Stone) and its detention for the benefit of the Republic and furthermore for the rendition of Services of the hands and the boat until it can be discharged each person shall be entitled to one-third league of land and the officers a proportionately larger quantity. You are not required to bear arms. . . . The Boat is not to leave without my orders.

The next day, from his "Camp West of the Brazos," Houston wrote the following commitment to the engineer of the *Yellow Stone*, Lewis C. Ferguson. Historian Eugene C. Barker, the editor of Houston's letters, has suggested that Ferguson may have required special inducement to move the steamboat.

I hereby bind myself to make title to one league of land [4428 acres], in consideration that he will act agreeably to my directions, and render to the army, all the aid in his power, as an Engineer, and officer of the Steam Boat Yellow Stone. And I do bind myself not to call on him to take arms in behalf of Texas, but will allow him to remain under the flag of the U. States, and its protection. The title [of the land] to made when the Boat is allowed to leave the Brazos River; and to land which I hold in my own right and property.

At this time Ross must have assumed that he would be ordered downstream, into the fury of enemy gunfire, or would be using his vessel to cross the army to the east side of the Brazos. To be safe he decided to protect the vital parts of his boat with the bales of cotton at his disposal. It was an easy idea to conceive, for the ordinary cotton packet was normally stacked high with bales on the main deck. "Fully loaded," says steamboat historian Alan L. Bates, "a cotton packet looked like an immense, floating cotton pile with stacks, pilothouse, and [wheels] being the only exposed parts of the boat. A passenger on a successful cotton boat could make an entire trip in the cabin without seeing the light of day." Ross made sure that the bales, which were capable of stopping rifle fire and even grape shot, were arranged to protect not only the boilers and engine on the main deck, but the pilothouse also.

A generation later, during the Civil War, the Confederate Navy used the term *cottonclad* to denote a vessel using baled cotton as armor, either when stacked on deck or packed between double bulkheads.

By the evening of 11 April, Ross was ready. He sent a note to Houston: "I think the Cotton we have on board necessary to protect the Boat & Engine — if we have to pass the Enemy's Cannon — I can transport 500 men with cotton enough to protect the boat from any damage from the Enemies fire . . . I can cross all the baggage without moving the cotton. I have four cords of wood on aboard & Every thing ready to 'go ahead'."

At the bottom of the note, Houston penned this endorsement: "Capt. Ross, All things will do as you say they are until further orders."

Houston was exhausted, bedeviled by his own indecisiveness and the dissension all around him. He had kept his own council, taken no advice, and obviously felt that something critical must happen soon. On the eleventh he wrote David D. G. Burnet, president of the newborn republic: "I am worn down in Body by fatigue, and really take my rest most in the morning, for I watch nearly all night, instead of being in a state of insanity I fear I am too irritable for my duties. . . . Our crisis is too important to indulge in any feeling but honorable emulation to save our country — I pity the man who loves office — God help him."

Before he could dispatch the letter, the word he and his men had been awaiting arrived. Santa Anna had reached San Felipe a few days earlier and learned, from a captured American, of Houston's location. Sensing no immediate threat from Houston, the Mexican general started looking for a way to cross the Brazos. In his own account of the campaign, Santa Anna wrote: "I immediately reconnoitered the bank of the river, right and left, for two leagues, hunting a ford by which to make a surprise by night, but all effort was fruitless. The breadth and depth of the river are great, it was swollen, and not even a small canoe was to be found."

After building two flat-bottomed boats and capturing other small craft, Santa Anna learned that Burnet and his government were in Harrisburg, about fifteen miles to the east. He decided to make a rapid march and attempt to capture these men. This news reached Houston in fragmentary form (he did not even know for sure that Santa Anna was personally commanding the column), but he learned enough to add this postscript to the letter he had just written Burnet: "News has just arrived that the enemy are crossing at Thompson's below Fort Bend. I don't know so well about it — I will cross the river soon and meet the enemy on the east side of the river if they are really crossing below."

At midmorning on 12 April, the firemen of the *Yellow Stone* had got up steam, carefully stoking their four cords of precious wood, keeping just enough pressure in the boilers to enable Captain Ross to cope with the current of the swollen river. The boat that had climbed the Missouri one wheel-turn at a time in low water, its screaming escapement pipe startling thousands of Indians, the boat that had made the newspapers from New York to Paris with feats of intrepidity, was now a giant raft.

Houston reported the successful maneuver to David Thomas, his acting secretary of war, the next day:

At ten o'clock A.M., yesterday, I commenced crossing the river, and from that time till the present (noon) the steamboat and yawl (having no ferry-boat) have been engaged. We have eight or ten wagons, ox-teams, and about two hundred horses, belonging to the army; and these have to pass on board the steamboat, besides the troops, baggage, &c. This requires time; but I hope in one hour to be enabled to be in preparation [to march].

———◇———

Safely across, having lost only one yoke of oxen, Houston got his men organized into a new regiment under Colonel Sidney Sherman. A couple of six-pounder artillery pieces called the "Twin Sisters" arrived, a gift from the citizens of Cincinnati. The paperwork began to flow, a sure sign of a functioning military organization. Orders of the day came from Houston's tent via the officer of the day, and undoubtedly were read to each company at morning parade. Sick calls went forward — there were some cases of measles in camp — followed by "sick reports." Company commanders brought their muster rolls and other company books up to date. Fatigue parties were organized, and everything was suddenly military again.

The regiment moved out. Despite some improvement in morale, many of Houston's followers found it hard to believe that he was marching *toward* Santa Anna at last. At a fork in the road, leading them inevitably to Harrisburg, it became clear to all that they were about to engage the enemy.

On 21 April 1836, a battle small in scope but great in outcome was fought where the San Jacinto River and Buffalo Bayou come together. Houston's army of about 700 defeated more than 1300 Mexicans, killing or wounding about 600 and capturing the rest, including Santa Anna. "Despite the small numbers involved," historian Archie P. McDonald has written, "the battle's consequences elevate it to consideration as one of the most significant military contests of modern man."

Houston released the *Yellow Stone* on 14 April as his army was clearing out of the Groce's Landing area. On the assumption that portions of the Mexican army were still on the river below, he gave a kind of passport to Captain Ross. He certified that the steamboat and crew had been detained "by order of the Commander in Chief, for the use of the Army of Texas," and declared that the officers and crew as citizens of the United States had been "expressly required to remain neutral" and had complied.

Encapsulated in cotton bales, stacked so high that only Captain Ross's head was visible above them in the pilothouse, the vessel headed downstream. She immediately began to pick up colonists who had left their homes during the Runaway Scrape.

There is no "official" account of the *Yellow Stone*'s pell-mell descent of the Brazos. The kind of raw material from which folklore is quickly woven, it has become the special favorite of

Sam Houston rides at San Jacinto in this painting by S. Seymour Thomas.

Texas newspapermen digging into the files for "sidebar" stories on Texas history. This is basically what happened:

Near Fort Bend, between San Felipe and Columbia, the *Yellow Stone* neared Thompson's Ferry where Santa Anna had crossed with his column. Mexican troops under generals Vicente Filisola and Joaquin Sesma were still in the area. They heard the steam pipe and the pulsing engine long before the boat came in sight, just as Kenneth McKenzie had once done while impatiently awaiting her arrival at Fort Union. When the vessel had bounced and bumped its way to within rifle range, the troops began to fire on her. Most of the Mexicans had never seen such a noisy monster and did not realize how impervious she had been made with her armor of cotton bales. Some artillerists tried to fire an eight-pounder at her, but that was a ridiculous gesture. So also was the alleged attempt to get a lariat around one of the chimneys.

Colonel Juan Altamonte, the Mexican chief of staff, had reportedly seen steamboats before and had told his troops to fire into the boilers. As these were concealed by the bales, and the two chimneys seemed to fit Altamonte's description, the men peppered those tall cylinders with musket balls.

An eyewitness said that "the boat, in making the turn of the bend below the ferry, struck the bank several times and turned completely around, and a merchant of Columbia named White who was aboard tried to get off on the bank." As the folklore began to build in later years, eyewitnesses would recall that the *Yellow Stone*'s whistle was sounding full blast. But she had no whistle, only the bell, and its wild tolling must have been considerably muffled by the barricade of cotton bales around it.

The *Yellow Stone* continued down to the Gulf and hastened to Galveston, where President Burnet and his Texas government — and hundreds of refugees — were staying. As the battle of San Jacinto had not yet been fought, and as no one could even say whether Houston was trying to engage Santa Anna or avoid him, these were nervous days on Galveston Island. Burnet held forth in the old customs house while an effort was made to fortify the island. Martial law was declared.

When word finally came that Houston had won the day, the *Yellow Stone* was making a brief trip on the Brazos, picking up goods at Quintana and Brazoria. Burnet got the news from Secretary of War Rusk by dispatch on 26 April; inclement weather and a poor boat had delayed the message until that time. Rusk asked Burnet to come to the San Jacinto camp immediately. The most logical conveyance was the *Yellow Stone*, now back in harbor but lacking the wood for a trip. Galveston Island was almost treeless, but wet driftwood was collected during the next four or five days; the steamboat reached camp on Buffalo Bayou about 1 May, carrying Burnet and members of his cabinet.

The battle had been fought on the cattle ranch of Peggy McCormick, and the Texans had declined to bury the 600 or so Mexican soldiers whose bodies lay strewn across Mrs. McCormick's grazing land. The odor of decaying flesh had forced the Texas troops to relocate further up the Bayou, nearer Harrisburg, and this is where the *Yellow Stone* reached Houston's headquarters. Lying wounded in his tent, for he had sustained a grievous wound in the ankle, was the victorious Houston, prepared to turn over control of the army and the prisoner Santa Anna to Burnet and the government of the Republic of Texas.

As Burnet and Houston had clashed many times and were in no way friends, the account that follows may be all or partially true. The *Yellow Stone* was being loaded for the return to Galveston under charter to the government. When an attempt was made to put Houston aboard, because he urgently needed treatment in New Orleans, Burnet turned him away with the claim that he was no longer entitled to government transportation because he was no longer in command of the forces. During the debate, the story goes, Captain Ross interceded and refused to pilot the *Yellow Stone* without Houston aboard.

The passengers on the trip to Galveston were an incredibly

S.A.S. ANTONIO LOPEZ DE SANTA-ANNA

Medals and gold braid were not enough to save General Santa Anna
when Houston's men caught him off guard.

mixed lot, a situation not unusual for the *Yellow Stone*. They included a suffering but victorious Houston, a president who despised him, the defeated leader of the Mexican army, and forty-seven captured officers and other soldiers under guard. The reminiscences of Pedro Delgado, a captured officer, include the claim that his fellow prisoners were made to sleep on deck "like bars of soap." Many a French *engagé* who had gone up the Missouri on the *Yellow Stone* could have understood that class of accommodation; it was called "deck passage."

Very early on the 8th, [Delgado continued,] after striking a bell three times, as is customary on these vessels, the machine was set in motion, and we glided down to Galveston. . . . As the steamboat passed opposite the battle field of San Jacinto, the troops on board were formed, facing to the field, and presented arms, the drums beating a march. They remained in that position until they had lost sight of the field. What was their object?

Lack of housing at Galveston prompted Burnet to move his office and his prisoners to Velasco within a few days. After taking these officials and probably Santa Anna to the place where preliminary negotiations with Mexico were to occur, the *Yellow Stone* was free to return to private commerce. Although she ran a few more errands for the army and the civil government, by 19 October her master, Thomas Wigg Grayson again, was publishing an ad in the *Telegraph and Texas Register*, reporting that when the stage of the river would permit he would operate between Quintana and Washington-on-the-Brazos. He was offering three dollars a cord for wood.

Months passed, and new officials took over the Republic. The crew of the *Yellow Stone* was attempting to collect on the promises made by Houston the General by sending a memorial to Houston the President. In May 1837 they wrote: "Your Memorialists . . . would respectfully call your Excellency's attention to the accompanying document — knowing your Excellency to be acquainted with the circumstances connected with the services rendered," and so on. It was signed by Ross "for himself and Crew."

Houston wrote the speaker of the Texas House of Representatives on 19 May:

I have the honor herewith to transmit to your Honorable body the memorial of Captain Ross, formerly of the Steamer Yellow Stone in behalf of himself and crew, a list of which is herewith annexed together with a copy of a letter addressed to him by the Commander in Chief of the Army on the 2nd day of April, 1836. I would respectfully recommend that the promise therein made shall receive your legislative sanction. When it is considered that our army was, at the time the promise was made, pressed on all sides by an overwhelming number of foes and without the possible means of crossing the river Brazos, save by the assistance of the boat under the command of Captain Ross, you will be able to appreciate the services rendered by the Petitioners and the propriety of fully complying with the undertaking which it was deemed necessary then to enter into, because, in as much as the boat's crew were all citizens of the United States, it was not within the power of the commanding officer to deliver them without the promise as was then made, and I do not hesitate to declare that the safety of our army depended upon the assistance of that Boat, there being no means within the power of the army to build boats to cross the river which was then very much swollen and remained so for some weeks.

That the facilities, derived from the Yellow Stone in crossing the Brazos, were great none can doubt, and had it not been for its services the enemy could never have been overtaken until they had reached the Sabine. I, therefore, beg leave most respectfully to solicit the interposition of Congress, to redeem the pledge which was made under the most pressing circumstances of our country.

In the years that followed, documents were scattered, another war with Mexico was fought, and Texas became a state. Historians generally assume that none of the claims was paid. Charlotte D. Ross, widow of the captain, filed a series of petitions in Harris County beginning 15 December 1853, stating that

Ross had died in 1848 and she wished to become his administrator. She declared he had a claim against Texas (now a part of the United States) "for his service, in crossing the Texas Army over the river Brazos in 1836 which will amount to nothing without an act of the legislature of the state."

On 8 December 1855, Houston wrote to Ashbel Smith, once the Texas secretary of state but now a state representative, hoping to get some action on Mrs. Ross's petition. "I believe Enmity to me has caused the delay of justice proven to him while living, and I pray it may not be withheld from his widow, when he is dead!" He repeated his avowal that the services of the *Yellow Stone* had enabled him to secure Texas:

What would a league of land have been worth, if I had been prevented from intercepting Santa Anna at San Jacinto? One hour short of the time that I reached San Jacinto would have enabled Santa Anna to have crossed the River, & formed a junction with the Indians who would of necessity have united with the Mexican army. . . . I think that this just claim should be paid to a widow whose husband rendered services to the country, which secured her Independence.

Houston enclosed a copy of the letter he had given Ross while preparing to cross the Brazos in pursuit of victory. Across the bottom of the letter he scrawled one more time the statement he had repeated so often: "A compliance on the part of Captain Ross and his crew enabled me to save Texas."

7

On Becoming a Legend

❧❡ STEPHEN F. AUSTIN was not the storybook image of a Texas pioneer. Small and lean, with fine features and a university education, he had a quality that many of his followers lacked. He understood the Mexican mind, the way that Mexicans loved to address all sides of a question warily and leisurely before attacking it head-on. His biographer, Eugene C. Barker, said of him that a topic could scarcely be so remote that Austin could not coax it into an argument "to further a favorite reform."

That is why Houston, Fannin, and Crockett did the fighting and Austin did the negotiating. Although he had talked unwary Mexican officials into opening the gates to American citizens, yet his persuasive ways were not always enough; the oblique approach was not infallible. He was to spend several months in Mexican prisons during the period of flaring anger on both sides that preceded the actual battle for Texan independence.

Historians who, as they must, are constantly revising the record of the past have produced some evidence that Austin was not always saintly in business matters, but no historian denies that Austin lived and breathed for Texas, gave Texas the breath of life itself, and made that vast land a substitute for wife and family in his zeal to see the dream realized.

Two *Yellow Stone* alumni may have met when this miniature watercolor on ivory was made about 1839 or 1840. The subject is Sam Houston and the artist is thought to be George Catlin.

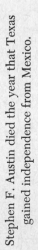

Stephen F. Austin died the year that Texas gained independence from Mexico.

His work in establishing the Americans in Texas was substantially done by 1832. Although he saw some early military action, he was away from his country doing what he did best when the Alamo fell, when the men of Goliad were betrayed and slain, and when Houston fell upon Santa Anna at San Jacinto. He was negotiating. Sent by the provisional government, he was a member of the commission authorized to arrange a loan with the United States and to ferret out, if possible, the attitude of the United States government toward annexing Texas.

When a permanent government for the new republic was formed in 1836, Austin was named secretary of state. But the rigors of imprisonment and many illnesses had made a near-invalid of the man who, at the age of forty-three, deserved to start enjoying the good life. He was staying in the home of Mr. and Mrs. George B. McKinstry, at Columbia, in late December when a visitor found him ill. He had come down with a cold, which everyone including his doctor thought would soon pass. It did not. His concerned friends brought him from his unheated bedroom to a pallet before the fireplace, where he seemed comfortable. Yet his condition worsened and he died on 27 December 1836.

George Hammeken reported that Austin's doctors gave him ipecac and tartar emetic in an effort to clear his lungs. "He would at intervals ask for a little tea," eyewitness Hammeken wrote later, "and during one of those intervals uttered his last words in a very faint voice. . . . Murmuring indistinctly, Austin seemed to say, 'Texas recognized. . . . Did you see it in the papers?' "

The patriarch has left us [proclaimed the *Telegraph and Texas Register* on 30 December]. We perform a most painful duty in announcing the death of General Stephen F. Austin, who departed this life on the 27th instant, at half-past 12 o'clock P.M. at the house of Judge McKinstry. . . . His remains left this place at 9 o'clock yesterday, followed by the citizens of Columbia and strangers generally, who were on a visit to the town, and was conveyed to the landing, and put on board of the steamboat Yellow Stone, which immediately left for Peach Point, the place of interment.

The destination of the entourage lay just a few miles down the Brazos, between Brazoria and Freeport. It was Peach Point Plantation, the home of Austin's sister Emily and her husband, James F. Perry. At this newly established country place, where Austin had designed a two-room wing for himself with a view of the bay, his body was taken to be interred in the plantation burial ground, Gulf Prairie Cemetery. "On arriving at Peach Point," the *Telegraph* reported, "the procession was met by a detachment of the first regiment of infantry, under command of Captain [M. K.] Snell, when funeral honors were paid to the illustrious dead."

The *Yellow Stone*, which had served Sam Houston in war, now had borne Austin on a last, peaceful voyage.

———◇———

The steamboat spent a month or so on the lower end of the Brazos and around Galveston, doing odd jobs. On 6 January 1837 she towed the schooner *Texas* up to the dock at Columbia. She hauled freight, as always, and a few military people. She made her first run to the new village of Houston, quickly rising along Buffalo Bayou. She was not the first steamboat to reach Houston, for the *Laura* had claimed that distinction. Exactly when the *Yellow Stone* first saw Houston is debatable, but it was in January or February 1837. There was some talk that the proprietors of the town might buy her, but she was too long and cumbersome to turn around in Buffalo Bayou. She had to back into White Oak Bayou to do that.

In the spring of 1837 the *Yellow Stone* was hired to carry a printing press into an area where communication was a vital need (she may already have taken a Mormon press to western Missouri in 1831; see page 25). The *Telegraph and Texas Register* was established in the fall of 1835 at San Felipe by Joseph Baker, Gail Borden, Jr., and his brother Thomas Borden.

This bell is thought to be from the *Yellow Stone*. Folklore says it lost its top when a piece was removed in the hope that the Liberty Bell in Philadelphia could be repaired with the metal.

It was to become the publishing facility of the provisional government, but not until it had been driven from town to town by the menacing Santa Anna. When the Mexican column bore down on San Felipe in March 1836, the publishers of the *Telegraph* quickly moved their press and its cases of type eastward to Harrisburg in wagons. The type was set and the forms "locked up" for the printing of the 14 April issue when the Mexicans approached Harrisburg. After six copies had been printed, Santa Anna's men arrived and dragged the press to the edge of Buffalo Bayou and tumbled it into the mud and water. The type, cast from a lead alloy, would have made effective grape shot for Santa Anna's artillery, and no doubt his men were too alert to waste the cases of type by letting them slide into the bayou with the press. As the first printing press had come to Mexico City in 1539, Santa Anna knew how the lack of one would disadvantage the Americans. Loss of the newspaper at Harrisburg was especially vexing to the provisional government, for the issue of 14 April was to contain important proclamations and documents, including "the executive ordinance, the only link unbroken, which, in the chain of government could hold Texas as a nation," as the editors later reported.

The owners went to Cincinnati in search of a new press, and a clue to the kind they bought is found in the description, "an old style Adam book press with wooden frame but iron bed and platern [platen]." Adam Ramage had been making presses of this kind in Philadelphia for more than twenty years, good pieces of equipment but not far removed from the kind used by Gutenberg in the late 1400s. In 1834, Ramage had switched to a press with an iron frame, and was selling it widely through the Cincinnati Type Foundry. It seems most probable that the Bordens and Joseph Baker had bought a trade-in with a wooden frame with which to reactivate the *Telegraph*, this time in Columbia.

When the newspaper was reestablished in the fall of 1836, it produced two important publications of the republic: *An Accurate and Authentic Report of the Proceedings of the House of Representatives,* and *Journals of the Senate of the Republic of Texas.* But since the little town of Columbia was finished as a capital and Houston was to become the seat of government, the publishers decided to move the publication for the fourth time. Recalling other difficult freightings by ox cart, this time they chose to ship their equipment on the *Yellow Stone.*

Gail Borden, Jr., was aboard, along with new editor and part owner, Dr. Francis Moore, Jr. They hoped to make a fast trip to Houston so they could put an issue of the *Telegraph* into the hands of subscribers without delay, but the vessel spent a week on the sandbar at Velasco, made a scheduled stop at Galveston, and got hung up on Clopper's Bar for another day. John James Audubon and his son, who had been exploring the bays and bayous that spring, were at Galveston on 25 April and saw the *Yellow Stone* depart for Houston with the United States revenue cutter *Crusader* in tow.

The steamboat eased her way up the Bayou to the Houston landing on 27 April. Next day, Sam Houston wrote his friend Dr. Robert Irion, "the S. Boat Yellowstone, 120 feet long, arrived yesterday with a cargo of goods and 140 passengers." The large list of passengers may indicate that on this trip the government itself — cabinet officers and other civil officials — were transported to the new capital.

Audubon and his son arrived in Houston on 15 May, in a rainstorm, and were welcomed aboard the *Yellow Stone* by James B. West, once the clerk but now the master of the boat. West turned his stateroom over to the Audubons so they might change into dry clothing, and invited them to dinner at the captain's table before they moved on. (On this stop, Audubon visited with Sam Houston, describing his large gray hat, velvet coat, and ancient cravat of the style of "seventy-six." Houston greeted him and his son warmly and offered them a drink.)

---◇---

At the end of May, the *Yellow Stone* was back in the Galveston area. Receipts and bills in the archives of McKinney and Wil-

Pioneering by steamboats like the *Yellow Stone*, the *Laura*, and the *Cayuga* made Houston a busy port. This vessel is of a slightly later time.

liams show that she was making deliveries of the usual necessities, including fish, pork, molasses, rice, and whisky. The last bill presented to the Texas navy department was dated 2 June 1837.

There is no further documentation of the vessel's existence in the McKinney and Williams papers, and no further mentions in the *Telegraph*. The New Orleans newspapers, which had been recording the arrivals and departures of the *Yellow Stone* in their shipping news for years, fell silent about the steamboat. No private letters have turned up saying, "I went down to Galveston on the *Yellow Stone*" or "We shipped our whole cotton crop to New Orleans on the *Yellow Stone*." There are no records of registry or enrollment at the port of New Orleans or any other port — at least none that have been found.

There is a single bit of evidence, all the more tantalizing because it stands alone. James Hall, a Cincinnati journalist who published promotional literature and statistics about the western states with unabating zeal, issued a work in 1838 entitled *Notes on the Western States; Containing Descriptive Sketches of Their Soil, Climate, Resources, and Scenery*. One of the tabulations presented by Hall is a list of vessels that passed through the Portland Ship Canal at Louisville in 1837. The *Yellow Stone* is there, with her correct tonnage and the toll of $86.44 paid to admit her through the locks.

If the steamboat did use the canal in 1837, it must have been after 2 June; her schedule would not have permitted a round trip during the earlier months of that year. A reasonable conjecture is that Thomas Toby & Brother sold her and sent her up the river to one of the industrial centers on the Ohio. If so, her name was changed, as there are no further enrollments on file in the National Archives for a vessel named *Yellow Stone* in that period. Another possibility is that she was scrapped, but after the extensive repairs she had received in late 1835, she was hardly ready for the scrap heap.

That version of what happened to the vessel is not the popular one, for it is little known. Thurman J. Adkins first called attention to the James Hall record in an unpublished master's thesis prepared in 1969. What most Texans believe, especially those who have visited the Alamo and seen the bell thought to have come from the deck of the *Yellow Stone,* is that the vessel was snagged and sunk, either in the Brazos or in Buffalo Bayou, depending on which bit of folklore is being quoted. It is a story that will not die, despite the many questions it raises. Why would not the sinking of such a well-known boat have been reported in the newspapers and written about in personal and business correspondence? A steamboat of this size, going down in the Brazos or the Bayou, would sit half submerged as a hazard or complete obstruction to navigation until removed. Yet the explanation is given some legitimacy in a compilation by William M. Lytle, first published in 1931 and now called *Merchant Steam Vessels of the United States, 1790–1868.* There the *Yellow Stone* is listed as having been snagged and sunk in the Brazos. But that listing was compiled long years after the fact, and no source of the information is given.

For those who are dissatisfied with these accounts of what may have happened to the *Yellow Stone,* there is yet another possibility. A hurricane occurred in the Gulf in the fall of 1837, causing great damage to shipping — especially in the Galveston area. When the storm began on 10 October, from twenty to twenty-five vessels in Galveston harbor lost their anchors or were blown onto the beach despite their anchors. Most buildings were damaged or destroyed, and there was fear that water would sweep over the entire island. In the words of one witness: "At daylight an awful scene presented itself to our view. Not a vessel, but one . . . but had gone ashore. Some high and dry, others had just reached the shore and were imbedded in mud and sand." In the confusion, with some vessels undoubtedly lost completely in the Gulf, it is possible that the *Yellow Stone* was a victim. It stretched credulity, of course, to suppose that she could have been in the area from June to October without leaving some written record.

Because the bell is there, the Alamo has been sanctuary to the fact and folklore surrounding the career of the *Yellow Stone*

Thomas Wigg Grayson brought the *Yellow Stone* to
Texas and was her captain during
part of her stay there.

in Texas. The library of the Daughters of the Republic of Texas, housed at the Alamo, contains newspaper items, reminiscences, unpublished manuscripts, and librarians graciously willing to answer any questions they can.

Here are some quotes from Texas newspapers, as clipped and saved by the staff:

The *San Antonio Express*, 21 June 1931:

When armed resistance to Mexico became the only recourse of the Texans, Captain [Thomas Wigg] Grayson offered his boat as a privateer for their services. In the Gulf he took many prizes, according to the records of the Yellowstone. And on April 14, 1836, he ferried the Texas troops across the Bayou as they took their positions for the Battle of San Jacinto.

The anonymous writer of this piece, delightfully inventive, told how the steamboat got her name:

It is said that on one of his many trips up-river, soon after acquiring the boat, Capt. Grayson went so far into the Northwest country — following the Mississippi, the Missouri, and the Yellowstone, that he got into the suddenly narrowed reaches of the upper Yellowstone and found that the only way out was to back out, which he did, ignominiously, for some miles. But he was so impressed by the beauty of that land of the Yellowstone that he decided to rechristen his boat, and from that trip until its final end in Buffalo Bayou, to everyone Capt. Grayson and "The Yellowstone" were synonymous.

The *San Antonio Express*, 25 November 1947: A story about the *Yellow Stone* says she chugged her way "nearly to the foot of the Rocky Mountains," and then the writer wonders "what she was doing so far south as New Orleans" when the war for Texas began. Again, the only captain mentioned is Grayson. By then an article was available in the *Waterways Journal*, a specialized periodical published in St. Louis for river workers and the shipping industry, and not likely to be seen by Texas newspaper writers. A piece in the issue of 5 April 1941 concentrated most heavily on the earlier career of the *Yellow Stone* and mentioned no other captain but Grayson.

In 1952 the Texas State Historical Society published its notable *Handbook of Texas*, edited by Walter Prescott Webb and others. Issued in two volumes, with a supplement to follow, it presented authentic Texas history in encyclopedic form. The article on the *Yellow Stone* by Sarah Groce Berlet, drawing upon her own research, identified Captain John E. Ross as master of the steamboat during the crossing of the Brazos. There was no longer much excuse for inaccuracy, since the *Handbook* became a part of the reference library of almost every newspaper in Texas.

Still, the *San Antonio Light* of 26 September 1954 ran a story on the famous bell in the Alamo, displayed beneath "a portrait of the seagoing San Antonian, Capt. Thomas W. Grayson, who commanded it during its gallant history of rescuing heroes of the revolution from the Mexican army."

It is probable that when the real fate of the *Yellow Stone* is discovered, the event will seem far less exciting than many of the occurrences in her short, turbulent life. Until that anticlimactic day, when some graduate student poring over old files in the Texas archives comes upon the simple truth, we are free to fantasize.

There is a legend of the sea that became the theme of Richard Wagner's *Der Fliegende Holländer* (or "The Flying Dutchman"). Author Frederick Marryat used the same theme in his novel *The Phantom Ship,* published in London in 1839. He relates the torment of Captain William Vanderdeken, who sailed in his ship the *Amsterdammer* for India in the seventeenth century. The captain declares,

For nine weeks did I try to force my passage against the elements round the stormy Cape [of Good Hope], but without success; and I

swore terribly . . . I blasphemed — ay, terribly blasphemed . . .
and I swore by the . . . Holy Cross . . . that I would gain my
point in defiance of storms and seas, of lightning, of heaven or of
hell, even if I should beat about until the Day of Judgment.

Vanderdeken's punishment for blasphemy was to struggle
until Judgment Day, trying to beat his way around the Cape,
never able to make port. He became known as the captain of a
ghost ship, the *Flying Dutchman,* and seamen thought that a
sight of the vessel meant doom for themselves.

And so to the *Yellow Stone.* It is a black night in the Gulf,
and she is trying to outrun a storm and reach safe harbor in
Galveston Bay. Or trying to cross the bar at the mouth of the
Brazos with the signal lanterns missing. Perhaps she is high up
the Missouri, aground in midstream throughout the night, a
prairie wind ripping at her topside and sandblasting the paint
from her chimneys.

She is a ghost ship, condemned for misdeeds aplenty: for
smuggling whisky to the Indians and paying them a pittance
for their season's catch. For becoming a slave ship twice a year
to carry *engagés* into the wilds for hard work and wretched food.
For harboring pestilence. For being a pioneering engine of
Manifest Destiny in the North and the South, toiling away in
the name of a people whose urgent vision of a nation united
sometimes blinded them to the dirty work that kept their dream
alive and their hopes moving westward.

No attempt has been made to annotate this volume beyond the occasionally general notes that follow.

GENERAL SOURCES. The literature on steamboating is large, but much of it does not apply here, dealing either with the invention and earliest days of steam transport or the later, so-called golden, age when the giant boats were plying the Mississippi and other inland waters. Works on steam travel in the West that have been helpful include Louis C. Hunter, *Steamboats on the Western Rivers* (Cambridge, Mass., 1949), alone in its field as a kind of compendium of the economics, mechanics, and lore of western steam travel. Hiram M. Chittenden, *The History of Early Steamboat Navigation on the Missouri River* (New York, 1903), delivers less than it promises, being mainly a biography of one pilot and captain, Joseph La Barge. George Byron Merrick, *Old Times on the Upper Mississippi* (Cleveland, 1909), is valuable for details of steamboat construction and the art of piloting. William E. Lass, *A History of Steamboating on the Upper Missouri River* (Norman, Okla., 1962), is useful, although the author defines the Upper Missouri as being that portion above Sioux City, Iowa. Any edition of Mark Twain's *Life on the Mississippi* is highly recommended.

Literature on the fur trade is also plentiful. A remarkable ten-volume set edited by LeRoy Hafen, *The Mountain Men and the Fur Trade of the Far West* (Glendale, Calif., 1965–72), contains biographical sketches of all the principals in the fur trade. Hiram M. Chittenden, *A History of the American Fur Trade of the Far West* (reprint, Stanford, Calif., 1954), is still a standard work, although originally published in 1902. David Lavender, *The Fist in the Wilderness* (Albuquerque, 1964), is primarily a biography of Ramsay Crooks, an important figure in the present work. Kenneth W. Porter, *John Jacob Astor, Business Man* (Cambridge, Mass., 1931), is an obvious and much-used source. Other books and articles are listed below where appropriate.

For the building and operation of the *Yellow Stone*, the basic source is the Chouteau Collection of manuscripts at the Missouri Historical Society, St. Louis. It may be assumed that specific information about the vessel and its operation, and the day-to-day business dealings of Pierre Chouteau, Jr., and the American Fur Company, are based on the documents in that collection. This superb archive is cataloged and, with some exceptions, arranged chronologically in sixty boxes of correspondence and a large number of ledgers, journals, and daybooks. Microfilming of the whole collection is now complete.

A master's thesis by Thurman J. Adkins, "Yellowstone: Biography of a Steamboat" (Trinity University, San Antonio, 1969), is an unusually well researched study from which I have benefited frequently. A copy is on file at the library of the Daughters of the Republic of Texas, in the Alamo.

CHAPTER 2 (pp. 28–50). The Chouteau Collection here and throughout the first five chapters.

The story of the Nez Perce quest is well covered by Alvin Josephy, *The Nez Perce Indians and the Opening of the Northwest* (New Haven, 1965), and has been supplemented by reference to Bernard DeVoto's constantly useful *Across the Wide Missouri* (Boston, 1947), and Chittenden's fur trade history.

For Catlin, a prime source is his own *Letters and Notes on the Manners, Customs, and Condition of the North American Indians* (2 vols., London, 1841). Easier to use is his biography by Harold McCracken, *George Catlin and the Old Frontier* (New York, 1959). Catlin's statement on his respect for Indians is from this work, p. 14.

On the delegation of Indians returning from Washington, the best source is John C. Ewers, "When the Light Shone in Washington," *Montana, the Magazine of Western History* 6 (Autumn

1956). Ewers cites or uses all other principal sources for this episode, including Catlin's *Letters*.

CHAPTER 3 (pp. 51–74). Paul Prucha, *American Indian Policy in the Formative Years* (Cambridge, Mass., 1962), Chapter 6, is the best concise treatment of the crusade against liquor for the Indians. David Lavender, cited above, presents an excellent narrative of the American Fur Company and its stand on liquor, drawing upon the Chouteau Collection.

The text of the Act of 1802 is in *United States Statutes*, 2:139–46. For the amendment of 1822, see *Statutes*, 3:682–83. For the Act of 1832, see *Statutes*, 4:564.

Correspondence among government officials, including the Secretary of War, Commissioner of Indian Affairs, William Clark and his subagents, is in the National Archives, Record Group 75, Office of Indian Affairs, Letters Received, St. Louis Superintendency. John Dougherty's comments on the search of the *Yellow Stone* and the Cabanné episode are in Record Group 75, Letters Received, Upper Missouri Agency.

For the vaccination episode, see the Act of 5 May 1832 in *Statutes*, 4:514–15, and Record Group 75. The story of the epidemic on the Upper Missouri has been told and retold, but see especially DeVoto's *Wide Missouri*, Chapter 11, and Annie H. Abel, ed., *Francis A. Chardon, Journal at Fort Clark* (Pierre, S.Dak., 1932).

A useful work, especially for the question of how smallpox was conveyed to the Mandans and Hidatsas, is Clyde C. Dollar, "The High Plains Smallpox Epidemic of 1837–38," *Western History Quarterly* 8 (January 1977). Dollar is skeptical about the transcript of Four Bears' speech at the time of his death, suspecting that it is a forgery.

Dougherty's letters to Secretary Cass on vaccination are in Record Group 75, Upper Missouri Agency, 6 June, 12 August, and 6 December 1832. The last named contains the reports of Doctors Davis and Martin. The report of Cass to Congress of 1 February 1833, containing Herring's statement on the vaccination program and several related appendices, is House document 82, 22d Congress, 2d session, U.S. serial 234.

CHAPTER 4 (pp. 75–96). The available edition of Maximilian's narrative is *Travels in the Interior of North America,* trans. by H. E. Lloyd, ed. by Reuben Gold Thwaites, in *Early Western Travels,* vols. 22, 23, and 24 (Cleveland, 1905). His field diaries are being edited for publication by William J. Orr and Joseph C. Porter, at the Joslyn Art Museum, Omaha, sponsored by The InterNorth Art Foundation and published by the University of Nebraska Press. A section of the diaries covering the party's travel along the eastern boundary of Nebraska in 1833 and 1834 has appeared in *Nebraska History* 64 (Fall 1983). Both these published sources have been used for the present work, as well as a typescript of the unpublished diaries.

For an article on the maps carried by Maximilian, see W. Raymond Wood and Gary E. Moulton, "Prince Maximilian and New Maps of the Missouri and Yellowstone Rivers by William Clark," *Western History Quarterly* 12 (October 1981). A work by William Goetzmann and a team at the Joslyn Art Museum has published *Karl Bodmer's America* (Lincoln, Nebr., 1984), containing reproductions of all his American works.

Pilcher's biographer is John E. Sunder, in *Joshua Pilcher, Fur Trader, Indian Agent* (Norman, Okla., 1968).

For an extensive history of Bellevue as a trading post, see Richard E. Jensen, "Bellevue: The First Twenty Years, 1822–1842," *Nebraska History* 56 (Fall 1975).

The Englishman Ashworth is mentioned in the John Townsend narrative, vol. 21 in *Early Western Travels,* pp. 197, 211, 220, 255, and 280.

CHAPTER 5 (pp. 97–117). Joseph La Barge's life story is told by Chittenden, *Early Steamboat Navigation.* For general background on the cholera epidemic of 1832–33, see Charles E. Rosenberg, *The Cholera Years: The United States in 1832, 1849, and 1866* (Chicago, 1962). The quotation from Isaac McCoy's journal is from Louise Barry, ed., *The Beginning of the West: Annals of the Kansas Gateway to the American West, 1540–1854* (Topeka, 1972), p. 238.

Nathaniel J. Wyeth reports on his visit to Kenneth McKenzie at Fort Union in Frederick G. Young, ed., *The Correspondence and Journals of Capt. Nathaniel J. Wyeth*, published in *Sources of the History of Oregon*, vol. 1, parts 3–6 (Eugene, Ore., 1899). McKenzie's diatribe against Wyeth and Cerré is in the Fort Union letterbook, Chouteau Collection, letters of March 1834.

The federal law of 30 June 1834, forbidding the distilling of spirits in the Indian country, is in *Statutes*, 4:729–35. The earlier law of 1815, much more specific regarding such distilleries, is in *Statutes*, 2:243–44.

Enrollment and registration papers of the *Yellow Stone* are in Record Group 41, Ships Registers and Enrollments, National Archives. These documents are reprinted in a publication of the Works Progress Administration, *Ship Registers and Enrollments of New Orleans, La.* (Baton Rouge, 1942), but in the December 1833 enrollment for the *Yellow Stone* the name of the owner, John P. Cabanné, is omitted.

The invoice for labor and materials used in refitting the *Yellow Stone*, submitted by Harrod & Hughes, is in the Thomas Wigg Grayson papers, library of the Daughters of the Republic of Texas, San Antonio.

CHAPTER 6 (pp. 118–138). Sources on the early days of Texas are ample. A fine account of those times is found in Ray Allen Billington, *Westward Expansion* (New York, 1974). The quotation from Billington is on p. 408 in that work. A brief but excellent account, Archie P. McDonald's *The Trail to San Jacinto* (Boston, 1982), is written mainly for undergraduates and based on primary sources.

Every researcher must start with *The Handbook of Texas*, edited in two volumes (Austin, 1952) by Walter Prescott Webb and H. Bailey Carroll, with a 1977 supplement edited by Eldon S. Branda. A multivolume edition is now being prepared by a staff at the Texas State Historical Society, Austin.

For early times on the Brazos, see Pamela Ashworth Puryear and Nath Winfield, Jr., *Sandbars and Sternwheelers: Steam Navigation on the Brazos* (College Station, Tex., 1976). For the firm of McKinney and Williams, see Margaret Swett Henson, *Samuel May Williams, Early Texas Entrepreneur* (College Station, 1976).

Specific correspondence related to the *Yellow Stone* and her crew in the days before the Battle of San Jacinto are in two sources. John H. Jenkins, ed., *The Papers of the Texas Revolution, 1835–1836* (Austin, 1973), is a ten-volume compilation of papers that suffers from lack of annotation, so vital in such a collection, and a poor index. It is, however, indispensable. Also valuable, but in need of re-editing, is the eight-volume collection, Eugene C. Barker, ed., *The Writings of Sam Houston* (Austin, 1938–43). Consult the index in James M. Day, compiler, *The Texas Almanac, 1857–1873: A Compendium of Texas History* (Waco, Tex., 1967).

Documents produced while the *Yellow Stone* was under Houston's control are to be found in the Jenkins edition. The later letters of Houston, as he attempted to obtain remuneration for the captain and crew, are in the Barker edition.

Recollections of the Mexican officer Delgado are in Pedro Delgado, *Mexican Account of the Battle of San Jacinto* (San Jacinto, Tex., 1919).

CHAPTER 7 (pp. 139–152). For the eyewitness account of Austin's death see George L. Hammeken, "Recollections of Stephen F. Austin," *Southwestern Historical Quarterly* 20 (1917), pp. 369–80. For the early history of the *Telegraph and Texas Register*, see Douglas C. McMurtrie, "Pioneer Printing in Texas," *Southwestern Historical Quarterly* 35 (1932), pp. 173–93. The story of Audubon's visit to the Gulf is told by Samuel W. Geiser, *Naturalists of the Frontier* (Dallas, 1948). The storm that struck Galveston in the fall of 1837 is described by Charles Waldo Hayes, *Galveston: History of the Island and the City* (Austin, 1974).

◄◄ APPENDIX A ►►

Construction of the Yellow Stone

In 1830, when Pierre Chouteau, Jr., arranged for the building of a steamboat in Louisville, it was customary to deal separately for the construction of the hull and its furnishings, with one contractor, and for fabrication of the engine with another. Chouteau contracted with William Crane and Company for the building of the hull, and with the Beatty & Curry Company for the engine. The Crane firm is not listed in the Louisville city directory for the period, and may have been located in one of the shipbuilding areas close by, as the contract speaks of the hull being "brought to Louisville." The Beatty & Curry foundry was a well-established institution in Louisville, located at the corner of Ninth and Water streets.

The contract for the building of the hull, presented and discussed here, named Jacob Beckwith the representative of the American Fur Company in supervising the work. Beckwith was an associate in the Beatty & Curry Company and may have helped Chouteau draw up specifications for the steamboat. None of his correspondence with Chouteau has been found. By the time the hull had been launched, supervision had passed to C. N. Halstead, whose periodic reports on progress are in the Chouteau Collection.

159

Halstead wrote on 6 March 1831 that the hull, then in the water, was the finest of its class that he had seen. It had been towed to the foundry landing and workmen would commence installing the engine the next day. Halstead said that a bell had been ordered from Pittsburgh and an anchor and chain from New Orleans. He assumed he was to hire the vessel's officers in Louisville, and he added this postscript: "Please write what name you intend giving the Boat."

About the middle of March, Halstead went shopping in Cincinnati for mattresses, curtains, and furniture not then available in Louisville. While the boat was being fitted out, Chouteau himself — undoubtedly on his way home from New York — stopped to inspect the work. Halstead wrote him 1 April, saying, "Since you left we have put Steam on the Engine." He added: "My prospects for fr[eight] & passengers is fair" for the voyage to St. Louis.

CONSTRUCTION OF THE HULL

As the terms of the contract are not self-explanatory to anyone but a student of steamboat history, the document below is followed by a few comments on the specifications. The reader is also directed to the glossary of steamboating terms in Appendix C.

[24 November 1830]

Articles of Agreement by & between Peter Chouteau Jr. Agt. Am. Fur Co. of St. Louis Mo. of the 1st part and Wm. Crane of Louisville of the 2nd part Witnesseth: That the said Crane agrees to build a steam boat of the following dimensions Viz: 120 feet in length on deck from the Aft side of her stern post to the ending of her Wales forward, 20 feet beam & 6 feet hold.

Her floor timber shall be from the stern as far as the builder finds it necessary in forming his frames to make them double with a space of 12 inches[,] four inches on the face & seven inches deep; from that place forward the floor timber shall be 6 inches face, the futtocks & top timbers 5 inches face, and 5 inches square at the head; the futtocks shall reach as high as a three feet water line & be let into the floors one inch. The frame 17 inches from center to center and extending from the aforementioned double frames to within 50 feet of the bow, where the double floor shall commence, which with the futtock shall be 4 inches face and on the top timber 5 inches face. The frames to continue 17 inches centers to within 30 feet of the bow when the space shall gradually lessen so as to arrive at a 2 inch space 15 feet from the bow to continue that space or less from that forward.

Her main & Engine Keelsons 7 by 9 inches, her bilge Keelson 8 inches square with good & substantial engine frames with 2 inch pine bulkhead on one side 45 & on the other 20 feet long & caulked, with snag room bulkhead well fitted & caulked. The boat must have good shoars under every beam with diagonal braces in the center & sides under the boilers & shafts. Her boiler & water wheel beams shall be 8 inches broad, her hatch beams and those under the Cylinder 4 inches broad, the balance of them 5 inches broad and all of them 6 inches deep, from the stern to the main hatch they may be made of pine or Yellow poplar & the balance of them of white oak 30 inches from centers. Her main deck & guards to be laid with 2 inch pine plank not more than 6 inches wide & caulked. The bottom plank 3 inches — deck decreasing in thickness 3 inches to 2 inches at the Wales. The planks above water must be well seasoned and not more than 8 inches wide and all her planks to average 40 feet long.

The forecastle must have 3 good breast hooks, must be lined & fitted for the crew to live in. The wheel rooms shall be 18 by 6 feet in the clear. The guard shall begin on the luff of the bow so as to make a fair line with the harping, and shall come in abaft the water wheel to about 3 feet wide, & go aft with a fair sweap, & finish with a round stern over the transom with a Nosing from the stern quite round. The cabin will be finished with 4 lengths of berths 3 open & one length in state Rooms, with a [ ] for a side board, & doors to open on the guards. The Cabin to be set in 18 inches so as to be 17 feet wide. Deck to be flush fore & aft and 17 feet wide & to extend forward so as to cover the forward hatch to be laid of seasoned pine plank 1-½ inch thick with tongues let in and laid in the same manner as the upper deck of the steam boat. Shank[?] with a railing to extend round it.

The side houses to be 12 feet long coming in as far as the outsides of the Cabin. The boat shall have officers rooms on the upper deck 12 feet long and 8 wide divided in two with bunks in each room, covered with inch boards groov'd & tongued with a good wheel house. The after guard to be covered with a light roof. All work not herein described appertaining to Shipwrights or Joiners work on steam boat to be performed free of extra charge by said Crane.

The materials for all the above mentioned work to be of the best kind and the work to be performed in a good workmanlike manner. The party of the 2nd part agrees to have said boat launched and ready to receive her Engine on or before the 1st March 1831 and to have all his work completed on or before 1st April following. The guards to be lined with 1 inch oak plank all round.

In all matters pertaining to the order of said work William Crane the party of the 2nd part shall adhere to the directions of Jacob Beckwith & in his absence to such person as he or the owners may appoint. The party of the 1st part agrees to pay the party of the 2nd part $1000 on 1st day December 1830 $500 when said boat shall be framed $500 when her main deck shall be laid $500 when she is ready to be launched, $500 when she is launched & brought to Louis-ville & the balance of $1000 when the boat is completed & ready for business. It is agreed by the parties that the boat and materials shall be held by the party of the first part as security for the same. In wit-ness whereof &c. 24 Nov. 1830.

Witness Present   Signed P. Chouteau, Jr.
J. W. Jolley   Agt. Am. Fur Co.
Jacob Beckwith   Wm. Crane

The weight and quality of the materials and the care with which Chouteau wanted them assembled are evident. Later in the steamboat era, when it became apparent that lighter wood meant shallower draft, and when statistics began to show that the average river steamboat — with a life span of about five years — was not worth the cost of fine workmanship, contracts were drawn with less attention to detail.

HULL AND HOLD

The contract calls for a hold six feet deep. While this indicates the amount of space available for storage, it is not the only factor in determining the depth of the hull in the water. The design of the hull, the total weight of the vessel, the actual lad-ing, all were factors. Pioneer river engineer Henry Shreve was later to declare that many of the boats on western waters were barely strong enough to hold the planking together and keep the caulking in place.

DECKS

The first or main deck held the engine and was the workplace of the vessel. Chouteau's contract calls for two decks, the second or boiler deck to serve as living quarters for the officers. In later times the boiler deck, with the ship's boilers beneath it, was to serve mainly as passenger quarters. On the *Yellow Stone,* before her modification in the fall of 1831, this deck provided officers' quarters and access to the pilothouse, but was not a complete boiler deck. The original plans were modified during construction to provide living quarters for the sailors or deckhands, because the forecastle on the main deck already had been designated for the firemen, who were presumably black. The *Yellow Stone*'s boiler deck was enlarged in the fall of 1831 to provide more passenger space, and the roof over this deck then became the hurricane deck. In no sense was the vessel ever more than a "two-story" steamboat.

SNAG ROOM

An empty compartment at the forward end of the hold, walled off by a heavy bulkhead, was built to prevent the flooding of the entire hold if the ship should be punctured by a snag.

SIDE HOUSES

Located just forward of the wheels on each side of the vessel, these structures were most frequently toilets. They were built partly on the guards, so that waste could go directly into the water.

CABINS

A cabin was not an individual sleeping room, but a structure containing several berths, private rooms, and a central hall in the center that served as a lounge and dining room. Packet boats were evolving into vessels with two cabins, the ladies' cabin aft as with the *Assiniboin.* Larger steamboats were built with cabins not only on the boiler deck but on the hurricane deck above.

PILOTHOUSE

This structure never emerges on the *Yellow Stone* as the fabled nerve center and command center of the vessel, as did those in which Mark Twain labored as a cub pilot. It was little more than a wheel to control the rudders, a series of signaling devices including bells and speaking tubes, and a weatherproof covering. In the illustrations of the *Yellow Stone* it is not shown perched high on the upper or texas deck, as in a later period. Rather, it is mounted forward of the boiler deck, and perhaps resting on that deck. The wheel operated the rudders by means of a rope that ran between the decks to the stern. If there was a fire aboard, the rope soon burned, leaving the boat unsteerable. The solution was the eventual replacement of the rope by a wire cable, and its constant grating as it was dragged back and forth in its pulleys beneath the passenger compartments became one of the irritants of steamboat travel.

GUARDS

Horizontal extensions of the main deck, serving as passageways and as added storage space for wood or freight, but designed originally to protect the wheels.

CONSTRUCTION OF THE ENGINE

Except for the paddles or buckets on the wheels, the spokes of the flywheel, and the long and powerful pitman rod, the engine was built entirely of wrought and cast iron. After a generation of experimenting, concepts first introduced by inventor Robert Fulton had been altered by Oliver Evans and others to the point that a western steamboat engine consisted of five features: a horizontal cylinder (the old ones had been vertical, introducing a great strain on the hull), a high-pressure steam cylinder, a simple valve system with a cam cutoff for economy, and a direct rather than condensing action in which the exhaust steam was vented noisily into the air.

The contract drawn between the American Fur Company and the firm of Beatty & Curry follows:

[24 November 1830]

Articles of Agreement entered into by & between P. Chouteau Jr. Agt. Am. Fur Co. of St. Louis Mo. of the 1st part & Beatty Curry & Co. of Louisville Ky. of the 2nd part. Witnesseth That the party of the 2nd part agrees to make & put up for the party of the 1st part an Engine of the following description: four boilers 16 feet long & 36 inches in diameter of Iron ¼ of an inch thick Cast Iron heads, & flues going through both ends, with Cylinder 20-½ inch in diameter & 5 feet stroke. The main shaft to be 8 to 8-½ inches at both Journals. The other parts of the Engine to correspond in size to those above discribed to be made of the best materials and in a good workman-like manner & to be put up complete on board the boat in 3 to 4 weeks after the boat is delivered at the landing in Louisville. The party of the 2nd part agrees to furnish one water wheel shaft, 2 flanges & 2 couplings extra & chains to support the water wheel beams. For and in consideration of the above work the party of the 1st part agrees to pay to the party of the 2nd part $1600 on 1st Decem. 1830 $1650 on 1st Feby. 1831 and the balance of $1650 when the Engine is put up & completed making in all $4950. In Witness whereof &c. 24 Nov. 1830.

P. C. Jr.
&
B. Curry & Co.

The principal parts of the *Yellow Stone* engine are discussed here briefly. The remarks may not apply to engines of later vintage in a rapidly developing technology. For a drawing of a similar engine, see page 5.

BOILERS

Placed side by side on the forward part of the main deck, these horizontal tanks were the heart of the engine. Steamboatmen never spoke of their vessels in terms of horsepower, but of boilers. "She's a four-boiler boat." Iron flues ran through the tanks, carrying hot gases that heated the water. Size of the tanks was dictated in part by the quantity of steam needed, and in part by a curious factor: the need for a slender worker to be able to crawl inside frequently to clean the mud and scale from the inner walls. Water was delivered to the boilers by a pump actuated by a paddle wheel in the early days. Later a small engine called a "doctor" performed this task. To avoid an explosion, the cold river water was preheated before being injected directly into the boilers.

CYLINDER

A piston traveling through the cylinder was driven in both directions, transmitting power to the pitman or connecting rod. It was fitted out with simple poppet valves, one steam and one exhaust valve at each end of the piston. A cam cutoff, first devised by Oliver Evans, cut off the flow of steam at half-stroke, more or less, allowing the natural elasticity of the steam to complete the stroke and thus save energy.

PITMAN OR CONNECTING ROD

A shaft of wood with metal fittings, extending perhaps fifteen feet from cylinder to wheel shaft, converting reciprocal to rotating motion and thus turning the wheels. One way of reversing the motion of a wheel was to change the way in which the pitman was connected; another method reversed the action of the valves.

WHEELS (PADDLE WHEELS)

The size of the wheels, averaging eighteen feet in diameter and six to eight feet in width, indicates the power needed to drive a vessel upstream against a current of four to eight miles an hour. In the beginning the wheels were placed almost amidships, but later they were moved somewhat forward. They were soon to be replaced by a single wheel at the stern.

FLYWHEEL

To even out the motion of the engine, keeping the application of power to the paddle wheels constant, a pair of twin flywheels was used. The cub engineer who "got hung up on dead center," with the flywheels stalled, felt the scorn of the captain and pilot at once. Because they were spinning rapidly in an unprotected area between the paddle wheels, they constituted a hazard to the crew.

The 1832 Roster

(24 March 1832)

A List of Men to be Employed by the American Fur Company to assist in the trade with the different Tribes of Indians in the Upper Missouri and to be transported on board of the Steam Boat Yellow Stone to their places of destination, viz:

MASTER
Bennett, Andrew G.

MATE
Berer, John

1ST ENGINEER
Newton, George

2D ENGINEER
Watson, Benjamin

PILOT
La Barge, Charles

STEERSMAN
Willis, John

SAILORS
Bronen, John
McDonald, J.
Scott, William
Silton, William

COOK
Scott, George

ASST. COOK
James

FIREMEN
Antoine
Harry
John
Joseph
Martin
Richmond

CABIN BOY
Calvin

TRADERS
McKenzie, Kenneth
Fontenelle, Lucien
Laidlaw, William

Lamont, Daniel

CLERKS

Bissonet, L.
Brazeau, Joseph
Brazeau, Duchouquette
Cerré, Pascal
Chardon, F. A.
Dougherty, John, Jr.
Halsey, Jacob
Kipp, James
Labone, Frederick
Laferriere, M. P.
Mitchell, D. D.
Papin, P. D.
Picotte, Henry
Primeau, E.
Sarpy, Thomas L.

INTERPRETERS

Campbell, Colin
Chapelle, L.
Degre, Charles
Dickson, Thomas
Dickson, William
Dorion, Baptiste
Dufond, B.
Primeau, Pierre

STEERSMEN [PATRONS]

Larriviere, P.
Thibeau, Alexis

BOATMEN [ENGAGÉS]

Albert, Chas.
Alliquier, N.
Barra, T.
Barada, Honoré
Becker, Frederick
Bergerand, P.

Bissonet, Bazile
Bourbonnais, Auguste
Bourke, Louis
Boydston, John
Boyer, Ph.
Brown, Wm. F.
Chaput, M.
Chatillon, Henry
Chatillon, Pierre
Champo, Pierre
Clermond, Louis
Cote, John B.
Crabb, John
Croteau, A.
Croteau, F.
Daigneau, F.
Daigneau, M.
Degueire, B.
Delile, F.
Demary, Louis
Derosier, Baptiste
Dionne, E.
Dubruille, A.
Ferland, Peter
Fecteau, F.
Fecteau, M.
Flures, Simon
Fry, Elias
Furse, Geo.
Galerman, A.
Gates, M.
Germain, P.
Girard, Fredk.
Gregoritz, M.
Grosclode, Justin
Grim, I. F. A.

Guinard, Alexis
Guinard, Louis
Guitard, Vincent
Harding, Eli
Hebert, Michl.
Henry, John
Hynes, John
Jackson, James
Jannot, Baptiste
Kamper, Tilman
Kuffler, Peter
Labuche, Nich.
Labusier, Louis
Laderoute, Ant.
La Fleur, Antoine
La Liberte, Jos.
Lalier, Mathew
Lambert, Geo.
Lemoire, Joseph
Lerou, Beralle
Lesage, John B.
Levaigue, P.
Licarre, Ralph
Looper[?], Michl.
Luck, John
Lukeman, A.
Marchand, J. B.
Marley, M.

Martin, Michl.
Menard, H.
Mist[?], William
Montaigne, F.
Monttruelle, P.
Morrin, Antoine
Morrin, Baptiste, Jr.
Morrin, Henry
Myer, John
Obermuller, Chas.
Obuchon, Louis
Palmier, Louis
Parision, Jos.
Peltzer, Frank
Poudrier, P.
Perry, Thomas
Perryeau, H.
Poirier, Jos.
Presse, Baptiste
Primo, B.
Robidoux, F. L.
Suprenant, M.
Traverse, Alfred
Vachard, Chas.
Valentine, Absolom
Valentine, Dennis
Wilson, Daniel
Witzcher, Fredk.

A Glossary of
Steamboating Terms

Not all of the following terms were in use during the 1830s, but all are encountered in the literature of the subject. Many are common to the language of seagoing mariners, while others were devised to fit the special needs of rivermen.

ARM. A spoke, as part of a paddle wheel.

ASH TROUGH. A metal pan beneath the grates, to catch ashes falling from the firebox.

ATHWARTSHIP. Across the ship from side to side.

BAR, SANDBAR. A riverbed obstruction of sand or gravel.

BEAM. Width of the hull, measured from inside the planking.

BELL ROPE. Line leading from the bell pull in the pilothouse to the engineer's position, or to a bell on deck.

BIGHT. A bend in the shoreline.

BIT, BITT. An anchor post on the forecastle for fastening head lines.

BLUFF REEF. A solid sandbar with a vertical side, so that deep water may flow close to the edge.

BOILER. Metal water tank in which steam is generated by heat passing through interior ducts.

BOILER DECK. The deck above the boilers, supporting a cabin area.

BOILER GUARD. A heavy frame on each side of the boiler area to reduce damage in an explosion.

BOOM. A timber supported by a mast and guys, used as a crane for moving freight or other objects.

BREECHING. Sheet-metal connector between boilers and chimneys.

BRIDGE. A platform forward on the upper deck; the station of the captain or master during landings and departures. A later development.

BRIDLE. An apparatus for holding the pilotwheel in place when the pilot must move away from it briefly.

BUCKET. The wooden blade of a paddle wheel.

BULKHEAD. An upright partition separating an area into compartments.

CABIN. An interior or enclosed part of the vessel on any deck, containing sleeping rooms and a common room.

CABLE. A heavy line made of manila rope.

CAPSTAN. A rotating cylinder on the forward area of the main deck, used as a winch for drawing lines. Operated by steam in later vessels.

CATWALK. A narrow walkway.

CHIMNEY. Early term for a smokestack.

COAMING. A curbing around the edge of a deck.

CRANK. A metal shaft attached to the pitman and paddle wheel shaft, changing linear to circular motion.

CUTOFF. A new channel formed when a river cuts through the neck of an oxbow bend.

CUTOFF VALVE. A valve gear designed to cut steam off before the end of the piston stroke. Full stroke was required only for maximum power, as in getting under way.

DAVIT. A crane for putting a lifeboat or other small boat in and out of the water.

DEADWOOD. A body of timbers built up at either end of the keel to provide a fastening for other supporting members of the hull.

DOCTOR, DOCTOR ENGINE. An auxiliary engine for operating pumps and doing other work while the main engine is shut down.

DRAFT. The depth to which the hull extends into the water.

DRAFT MARKS. Numbers painted on the hull to indicate draft.

ESCAPEMENT OR ESCAPE PIPE. A pipe exhausting steam into the air above the top deck.

FALLS. A set of blocks and tackle.

FANTAIL. The part of the main deck extending aft of the hull.

FENDER. A pad to prevent parts of the boat from rubbing against other objects.

FIREBOX. The compartment in which wood is burned to heat water in the boilers.

FLANGE. The hub of the paddle wheel to which the arms are attached.

FLUE. A duct conveying heat from firebox to boiler, and into the chimney.

FORECASTLE. The fore part of the main deck, often used as quarters for crew.

FREEBOARD. The distance between the guards and the waterline.

GANGPLANK. A plank extending from main deck to shore, or from boat to boat. If suspended by lines, it is called a stage.

GRASSHOPPER. A verb, meaning to move a vessel out of a shallow area by means of spars operated by the capstan.

GUARD. The portion of the main deck extending beyond the hull.

GUNWALE, WALE. The upper edge of the hull. The gunnel.

GUY, GUYWIRE. A line or wire that steadies a boom, mast, chimney, or other part of a vessel.

HARPING. The upper contour or outline of the hull.

HATCH. An opening in the hold through which cargo is passed.

HAWSER. A manila line used in mooring or towing.

HOG CHAIN. An iron rod or chain passing over struts from bow to stern, to improve rigidity and prevent the sagging of the hull. Not used on the *Yellow Stone*.

HOLD. The space enclosed by the hull, generally for cargo.

HURRICANE DECK. In the early period, the deck above the boiler deck. Now the lowest roofed deck.

HULL. The shell or main body of a vessel.

ICE SHIELD. Metal sheathing on the hull, protecting the bow from ice both above and below the waterline.

JACKSTAFF. A mast at the bow from which an emblem or insignia is flown.

KEDGE, KEDGE ANCHOR. A small anchor dropped ahead of a ship, to pull it forward by means of a line.

KEELSON. A line of timbers laid over the keel, to which the floor timbers are fastened. The bulkhead running fore and aft in the center of the ship. Pronounced "kelson."

KEVEL. An iron or wooden cleat attached to a deck, for fastening lines.

KNEE. An angular timber fastening the beams of the hull to the sides or timbers.

LEAD, LEADLINE. A weighted cord marked off to determine water depth.

LINE. Any rope, cable, or wire, or any pipe on a vessel.

MAIN DECK. The first deck, upon which the boiler and engine are installed.

MANHOLE. An opening in a boiler from which it may be inspected or cleaned.

MAST. Any upright timber or pole.

MUD CLERK. Assistant clerk whose duties ashore often gave him muddy feet.

MUD DRUM. A container beneath the boilers to collect sediment.

OXBOW. A U-shaped river bend that has produced a narrow neck of land that may eventually be cut through by the current.

PACKET BOAT. A vessel for hire, carrying passengers and freight, and perhaps mail, equipped for overnight trips.

PADDLE WHEEL. A wheel fitted with paddles or "buckets" that propels a steamboat.

PAINTER. A light line used to secure a small boat.

PILLOW BLOCK. The support for a shaft bearing.

PILOTHOUSE. A compartment atop the texas, usually aft of the chimneys, from which the pilot steers and directs the vessel.

PITMAN ROD. A rod connecting a vibrating element to a rotating one. Hence, the rod connecting the piston with the crankshaft between the paddle wheels.

PLANTER. A snag that has one end fixed in the riverbed.

POINT. An arm of land extending into a river, affecting the current and creating a sandbar.

PORT. The left side of a ship, looking forward.

REACH. A straight stretch of river.

ROSIN. A powdered forest product, made by the distillation of turpentine, used in the firebox to aid the combustion of wet or green wood.

RUDDER. The hinged fin or plate at the stern that governs the direction of a vessel's movement.

RUDDER POST. A vertical member that holds the rudder.

RUNNING LIGHTS. A pair of lanterns, one red and one green, mounted high on the chimneys as navigational aids for other vessels.

SAFETY BARGE. A boat towed by a steamboat to provide a means of escape for passengers and crew in case of accident.

SAWYER. A tree fastened in the riverbed, its trunk and branches bobbing or sawing in the stream.

SCANTLING. A board used in framing; thus, any board not considered a plank.

SCAPE PIPE. Escapement pipe.

SCUPPER. A deck drain.

SHEER. The curve of the deck as viewed from the side.

SHOAL, SHOAL WATER. Shallows, or water of little depth.

SKEG. A fin placed ahead of the rudder to prevent lateral motion of the hull.

SKYLIGHT. A row of windows or transoms at the top of a cabin to allow for sunlight and ventilation.

SLOUGH. A side channel or inlet from a tributary of a river.

SOUNDING. A measurement of water depth, often called out to the pilot by the mate or other crewmen.

SPAR. A substantial wooden pole or timber with many uses, including the sparring or "grasshoppering" of the vessel out of shoal water.

SPEAKING TUBE. A line of pipe connecting the pilothouse and engine room. Gutter pipe was normally used.

STACK. The smokestack, formerly called a chimney.

STACK LANTERN. A running light.

STAGE. A platform or gangplank serving as a bridge to shore during landings, especially one suspended by lines.

STANCHION. An upright brace supporting a deck, rail, etc.

STARBOARD. The right side of a ship, looking forward.

STATEROOM. A sleeping compartment for officers or passengers.

STIRRUP. A double bolt, with nuts, that clamps the paddle or bucket to the arm of the paddle wheel.

STEERSMAN. A sailor who operates the wheel in the pilothouse, subject to the commands of the pilot.

STEM. A timber to which the sides of the hull are joined at the bow.

STERN. The rear part of the hull, to which the rudder is hinged.

STRIKER. An apprentice crewman, especially an engineer.

STROKE. The distance traveled by the piston during one complete revolution of the wheel.

TEXAS; TEXAS DECK. The texas (never capitalized) is the topmost cabin, usually for officers, which rests on the texas deck.

TILLER. A horizontal lever that turns the rudder.

TILLER ROPE. A line attached to the tiller by which the rudder is controlled from the pilothouse.

TORCH BASKET. A metal container on a pole, hung at an angle over the water and containing burning wood chips or other fuel for nighttime illumination, especially at landings.

TOW. A vessel or barge being pushed or pulled by another boat. Verb, to tow.

TOW-HEAD. An island covered with thick vegetation, such as willow or cottonwood saplings.

TRANSOM. The frame or vertical planking at the stern of the hull.

TREE NAIL, TRENNEL. A wooden spike or dowel used to fasten timbers together.

'TWEEN DECK. A low deck between the main and boiler decks, carrying passengers or freight. The *Assiniboin* had one, but the *Yellow Stone* did not.

WHEELHOUSE. The casing around the paddle wheel on a side-wheel vessel.

WIND REEF. A pattern on the surface of the water, created by the wind, simulating the presence of an underwater reef.

WOOD BOAT. A barge carrying cordwood, meeting steamboats on a prearranged basis to speed up refueling.

WOODHAWK. A riverside woodcutter, offering cordwood for sale to passing steamboats.

YAWL. A small boat, towed or carried.

INDEX

YS is the abbreviation for *Yellow Stone*. Some names of persons and places occurring routinely are omitted.

Lee, Rev. Jacob, 33
Lemoire, Joseph, 169
Lerou, Beralle, 169
Lesage, John B., 169
Levaigue, P., 169
Lewis, Meriwether, 55
Lewis and Clark Expedition, 23, 32
Lexington, Mo., 14, 15, 112
Liberty, Mo., 14
Liberty, steamboat, 4
Liberty Landing, 84
Licarre, Ralph, 169
Light, the, an Assiniboin: trip to East Coast, 42–45
Linn, Dr. Lewis F., 101
Little Cheyenne River, 46
Little Sioux River, 19
Long, Maj. Stephen H., 20
Looper[?], Michl., 169
Louisville, Ky.: steamboat center, 1, 3, 147; YS built at, 3
Lovejoy, [————]: engineer, 6
Lubbock, Thomas, 127
Lubbock, Francis W., 127
Luck, John, 169
Lukeman, A., 169

McCormick, Peggy: and site of San Jacinto battle, 134
McCoy, Isaac, 102
McDonald, Archie P.: quoted, 131
McDonald, J.: deckhand, 167
McKenzie, Kenneth: trader, 3, 22, 167; forms Upper Mo. Outfit, 11–12; and distillery, 103–8; visits Europe, 109
McKinney, John, 127
McKinney, Thomas F., 120
McKinney and Williams, 120, 121
McKinstry, George B., 141
McLain, M. M., 127
Maguire, George, 56
Man of the Morning, a Nez Perce, 32
Mandan, steamboat, 20
Mandan Indians: Catlin's view of, 46–47; and smallpox epidemic, 68–71
Marchand, J. B., 169
Marion, Tex., 120
Marley, M., 169
Marryat, Frederick, 51
Martin, Michl., 169
Martin and Askin: own YS, 112
Maximilian, Prince of Wied: on YS, 79–96; illus., 78; as scientist, 79; biog., 79; at New Harmony, 79; and Lewis and Clark maps, 80; and U.S. scenery, 83–84; and natural history, 86, 87, 89; describes Omahas, Poncas, 90, 91; criticizes Catlin, 92–93; leaves YS, 96
Menard, H., 169
Mexican Federalists, 120
Mills County, Iowa, 87
Missouri, steamboat, 4
Missouri Republican, newspaper, 50

Missouri River: described, 19
Mist[?], William, 169
Mitchell, D. D.: clerk, 168
Mitchill, James: deckhand, 8
Mobile Grays, 121, 125
Monona, steamboat, 4
Montaigne, F., 169
Monttruelle, P., 169
Moore, Dr. Francis: publisher, 145
Moreau River, 46
Morgan, Dale: quoted, 42
Mormons: migration of, xvi; in Missouri, 25, 142; publications of, 25
Morrin, Antoine, 169
Morrin, Baptiste, Jr., 169
Morrin, Henry, 169
Mosely, Mr. and Mrs. Robert, 127
Myer, John, 169

New Orleans, La., 112, 113, 115, 133, 147
Newton, George: engineer, 167
Nez Perce Indians: and quest, 31–35
Nicollet, Joseph N., 18, 30
Nimrod, steamboat, 6
Nishnabotna Narrows, 87
No Horns on His Head, a Nez Perce, 32–35; portrait, 35

Obermuller, Charles, 169
Obuchon, Louis, 169
O'Fallon, Benjamin: and Clark maps, 20
Old Three Hundred, the, 119
Omaha, Neb., 19, 88
One Horn, Sioux chief, 39
Otto, steamboat, 103

Palmier, Louis, 169
Papin, P. D.: clerk, 168
Parision, Joseph, 169
Parkman, Francis, 30
Peach Point Plantation, 142
Peltzer, Frank, 169
Perry, Emily, 142
Perry, James F., 142
Perry, Thomas, 169
Perryeau, H., 169
Petre, Touissant: steersman, 8
Phelps, William A.: and Mormon press, 25
Phillips, John P.: owns YS, 112
Picotte, Henry: clerk, 168
Pigeon's Egg Head. *See* Light, the
Pilcher, Joshua: trader and agent, 31, 41, 54, 69, 88, 103
Pilot: duties of, 7–8
Pirate, steamboat, 112
Pittsburgh, Pa., 104
Platte River, 19
Poirier, Joseph, 169
Ponca Creek, 20
Ponca Indians: described, 91–92
Ponca Post, 12